The Emerging BLACK GOP Majority

Earl Ofari Hutchinson

Copyright 2006

Middle Passage Press
5517 Secrest Drive
Los Angeles, CA 90043

Publisher
Middle Passage Press
5517 Secrest Drive
Los Angeles, CA 90043

Publisher's Cataloging-in-Publication
(Provided by Quality Books, Inc.)

Hutchinson, Earl Ofari.
    The emerging Black GOP majority / by Earl Ofari
Hutchinson.
    p. cm.
    Includes bibliographical references and index.
    ISBN 1-881032-19-1
    ISBN 1-881032-20-5

    1. African Americans--Politics and government.
2. Republican Party (U.S. : 1854-)   3. Party affiliation--
United States.   I. Title.

E185.615.H88 2006   305.896'073
                                      QBI06-600115

Other books by Earl Ofari Hutchinson

The Crisis in Black and Black

Beyond O. J.:
Race, Sex and Class Lessons for America

The Disappearance of Black Leadership

Blacks and Reds:
Race and Class in Conflict, 1919-1990

Betrayed: The Failure of the
Federal Government to Protect Black Lives

The Assassination of the Black Male Image

Acknowledgments

S pecial thanks to Barbara Bramwell Hutchinson, Jasmyne Cannick, and Martha Nichols for their crucial insights and suggestions.

I also owe a deep debt of gratitude to Democrat and Republican analysts, strategists, and critics who offered their thoughts and encouragement. It was truly a bipartisan effort. *The Emerging Black GOP Majority* could not have emerged without their generous support.

Table of Contents

Introduction

"We're the freest black folks that have ever been in anyone's administration." The words from Alphonso Jackson, President Bush's Secretary of Housing and Urban Development, were bold, brash, and pugnacious. Without calling any names, Jackson almost certainly was responding to the relentless nonstop criticism from civil rights leaders and black Democrats that Bush's black appointees were showpiece pawns of the Republicans and that they had absolutely no power.

Jackson made the comment in a talk with a black reporter in Pittsburgh in March 2006. He was in town to ladle out millions for a new Bush administration low-income housing initiative. But housing was less on Jackson's mind than the charge of political cronyism leveled against the black Republicans. During the interview he repeatedly went back to it.

That charge stirred fierce national debate in July 2004. At that year's NAACP convention, then-NAACP President Kweisi

Mfume tore into President Bush's black supporters, calling them "ventriloquist's dummies." In articles and on conservative TV and radio talk shows, a slew of them had passionately applauded Bush for rejecting an invitation to speak at the NAACP's annual convention. Mfume was teed off — not just at their defense of Bush, but also that there were so many of them willing to defend him. Within days after his public bashing, the Bush–Cheney re-election campaign website announced the formation of the African-Americans for Bush Leadership Team.

The 76 members listed on the National Steering Committee are businesspersons, professionals, ministers, and state and local elected officials. With the exception of former Oklahoma Congressman J. C. Watts, who headed the committee, none were well known, but many of them lived in the crucial battleground states of Pennsylvania, Michigan, Missouri, Florida, Ohio, and Wisconsin.

They couldn't be brushed off or ridiculed as the usual assortment of black Republican operatives, conservative think tank ideologues, or high-profile talk show hosts who are committed Bush loyalists. These were public-spirited individuals motivated solely by their belief in Bush's policies..

Bush's African-American team was a calculated effort to bypass mainstream civil rights leaders and cultivate a new brand of black leadership. That effort was driven by political necessity, idealism, and opportunism. His court-and-shun technique in his relations with blacks reflected the GOP's century-old dilemma: The party needed black votes but feared that by openly courting blacks it would alienate white voters, especially white Southerners. In the early decades of the Twentieth Century, the GOP waffled on anti-lynching legislation, and in later years warred against big government, entitlements, welfare, and affirmative action.

The party's foot dragging — and at times, outright antagonism to civil rights legislation — angered civil rights leaders and tagged it as racist — insensitive and racist — and a permanent pariah with civil rights leaders. The only recourse was to skirt the traditional black leadership and create a visible, conservative, and activist leadership that could go head to head with civil rights leaders and push GOP policies.

That new leadership would come from the ranks of the post-civil rights generation. The younger business- and profession-oriented blacks in that group were more prosperous, more secure, and more disenchanted with the Democrats than in past times. A significant percentage of the young, prospering blacks called themselves *political independents* and even *conservatives*. Polls consistently showed that a significant number of blacks favor stiffer sentences for drug use, violent crimes, and three-strikes laws, and a near majority support the death penalty and school vouchers. Other polls showed that the majority of blacks backed welfare reform as a way to end dependency and encourage personal initiative.

Their political moderation opened up fresh possibilities for the GOP. The spectacular emergence of the black evangelicals as a potent political force was energized by the GOP's anti-abortion, anti-gay rights, and pro-school prayer pitch. In the battleground states, the fresh crop of celebrities and politically connected, cash-rich black senate and gubernatorial candidates offered promise to put a fresh and dynamic face on the GOP's racial thrust.

Bush and GOP strategists believed that they stood on a historic threshold with a real shot at breaking the Democrats' half-century grip on the black vote. That breakthrough would assure the GOP political supremacy in national politics for years to come.

Towering barriers were still in the party's path: the implacable enmity of civil rights leaders; Bush's snub of the NAACP; his Katrina fumble; racist gaffes by some Republicans and the silence of top GOP officials concerning them; and the repeated charge that the Republicans engage in dirty tricks in the 2000 and 2004 elections to suppress the black vote. Then there's the biggest obstacle of all, and that's the ingrained perception that the party is run by shot-caller, rich, white guys who are inherently hostile to black interests.

That notion deeply worried Free Congress Foundation head Paul Weyrich. Weyrich, whose ultra-conservative credentials are impeccable, openly groused that Republican leaders talked out of both sides of their mouths when it came to support of the top black GOP candidates for Senate and gubernatorial spots in the fall 2006 elections. Publicly, they praised them; behind the scenes, they bad mouthed them as poor candidates, tightened the funding purse strings on them, and even coaxed white candidates to run against them in the primaries in a effort to subvert their candidacies. ("It remains to be seen if Republicans at the grassroots level are ready for black Republicans to be elected. I'm not sure they are.")

The fear and loathing many blacks have had in the past half century of GOP policies guaranteed Democrats a perpetual upper hand in the hard-fought bid for black voters. In fact, such black conservatives as anti-affirmative action crusader Ward

Connerly believed that Katrina had irreparably damaged Bush: "Politically, there went the ball game for the GOP outreach effort to attract a greater number of blacks to the GOP." Despite the apparent hopelessness of it, Republicans could not afford to completely throw in the towel in the hunt for more black votes. Bush had publicly pledged to be a "compassionate conservative" and make the party more diverse than it had been in the past half century.

He and the GOP could not completely renege on that pledge no matter how bad his post-Katrina racial reversal of fortune. Even if the GOP had no real chance to ever create an emerging black GOP majority, it still had to try.

Chapter 1

The Emerging
Black GOP Majority

Six days before Christmas in 2005, a confident-sounding President Bush fielded questions at a White House press conference on the deadly and chaotic turmoil in Iraq, the brewing controversy over his domestic spy program, and the ups and downs in his war on terrorism. Bush's confident tone vanished the instant a reporter asked him what he was giving to the nation on the issue of race. It was the type of left-field question on which Bush had often stumbled and bumbled in the past.

It was no different this time. A defensive Bush lashed out at those critics who pummeled him for being indifferent to

1

racial issues. However, it wasn't just generic racial matters that Bush had in mind while answering his detractors — it was his soured relations with African-Americans. In early September 2005, hip-hop superstar Kanye West stunned a crowd at a nationally televised Hurricane Katrina relief telethon (on NBC) when he departed from the script and charged, "George Bush doesn't care about black people." West took some public heat for his jab at Bush, and NBC executives and sponsors quickly distanced themselves from his remarks. He stuck to his guns, though, and said that he had expressed the anger many blacks felt toward Bush in the wake of the Katrina horror.

At the White House press conference, Bush said that he was hurt and offended that anyone could think that he was callous toward blacks and rambled off a list of things he had done: more home ownership, support of minority business, his plan to privatize social security (by then virtually defunct), and the creation of more jobs. He punctuated his defense by assuring that he'd sign the Voting Rights Act extension in 2007. Buried in his disjointed litany of racial accomplishments, Bush also promised that he would and could do a better job toward blacks.

This wasn't a backdoor admission of personal or political failings on the part of the president. He quickly added that he meant that he had only done a lousy job in communicating his administration's accomplishments to blacks. Bush seemed to think that if he put a fire under his communications people and got them to churn out more and better press releases, everything would be fine. That was a delusion. The stark reality was that more blacks than ever not only opposed the president's policies but personally loathed him.

An NBC–*Wall Street Journal* poll in October found that Bush's popularity rating among voting blacks had plunged to an eye-popping, head-shaking low of 2 percent. The low was so mind-boggling that incredulous NBC political analyst Tim Russert screeched to NBC anchor Brian Williams "only 2 percent!" That figure would've made Bush the most unpopular president among blacks in the history of American poll-taking. However, an ABC poll that showed his mind-boggling low support from blacks was almost certainly inaccurate. A later poll by the more authoritative Pew Research Center seemed to spare Bush a repeat of his previous embarrassment. It pegged the drop in his approval rating from 14 percent down to 12 percent. That was more modest and comforting for the White House.

Bush's poll free-fall or dip was chalked up to his comatose response to Katrina disaster relief and his walk-on-eggshells reaction to a crack made by conservative talk show commentator, former President Reagan's Education Secretary William Bennett, in September 2005: Bennett said that aborting black babies would reduce the crime rate. When a defiant Bennett refused to back away from his foot-in-mouth racial slur, Bush remained mum. Whether Bush actually skidded to rock bottom or simply skidded in the ratings mattered little — his popularity drop in the polls was a stunning and savage reversal of fortune that few presidents have experienced in modern times.

Five months before his popularity plunge, a packed audience of black business leaders, clergy, veterans, black congresspersons, Mel Watt (Chair of the Congressional Black Caucus), and Illinois Senator Barack Obama interrupted to applaud Bush 17 times during his fifteen-minute speech in the White House's East Room. A pumped up Bush pledged that he'd vigorously enforce laws against discrimination in housing, education, and public accommodations: "We'll continue working to spread hope and opportunity to African-Americans with no inheritance but their character."

This was a naked reference to Dr. Martin Luther King Jr.'s famed line in his March-on-Washington speech in 1963 in which King begged America to put character before race as the standard for judging black progress. Bush's use of King's color-blind society plea struck a chord with the participants. The presence of such top black Democrats as Watt and Obama was further proof that Bush had indeed touched a nerve with some black voters. They felt that they had to at least hear what Bush had to say about black issues. Bush had staked a part of his and the GOP's future on bagging more of the black vote than anyone ever thought possible. Bush had the momentum, and he wasn't about to let it slow.

GOP leaders stepped up the pace in their push to get black votes. In July, Republican National Committee chair Ken Mehlman spoke at the NAACP's convention and got a fairly cordial greeting. Considering the five years of frozen relations between the Bush administration and the NAACP, that was a big step forward for him. Bush had the dubious distinction of being the first sitting president in nearly a century to refuse to address an NAACP national convention.

At the convention, Mehlman did a mea culpa for past GOP racial slights and swore that the party would do whatever it took to make amends for them. Meanwhile, a few hundred miles away, his boss got an equally cordial greeting at the Indianapolis Black Expo. Bush enthusiastically pumped up his program for jobs, minority business, and homeownership. He again pledged to do whatever he could to make the party even more inclusive. That message struck a chord with many upwardly mobile young black professionals and business-persons.

Hip-hop mogul Russell Simmons was one of those smitten with the president's message. In an interview on MSNBC's Hardball, Simmons impishly gushed that he had had such fun in a private meeting with Mehlman that he didn't make it to a scheduled meeting with Democratic National Committee Chairman Howard Dean (a spokesman for Dean said no such meeting was scheduled). If Mehlman could yuck it up with a top hip-hopper, maybe Dean should have scheduled a meeting, too. The Simmons and Mehlman duet caught the attention and worry of NAACP's Political Director, Hilary Shelton: "People like Russell Simmons are smart enough to understand the impor-tance of sitting down with all players in politics."

A scant two months after his Indianapolis triumph, the months of planning, calculating, maneuvering, and promises — not to mention the millions Bush, Mehlman, and Republican strategy guru Karl Rove spent on their minority outreach — Katrina had seemingly brought things to a grinding halt, if not a thundering crash. Yet, it did appear for a time that Bush had done the unthinkable and had rocked the Democratic Party back on its haunches with his black-voter-outreach campaign. That was unthinkable only because for the past half-century, blacks have been granite solid Democratic loyalists. The Demo-crats received 80 to 95 percent of the black vote in every election since Lyndon Johnson's landslide victory over Barry Goldwater in 1964. They have received little in return. The black poor are more numerous. They live in crime- and violence-plagued neighborhoods. Their children attend miserably failing public schools. Public services in their communities are abominable.

Top Democrats saw the danger to their party caused by decades of neglecting the interests of the black community and, by extension, black voters. The danger lay in the Republican offensive to capitalize on that neglect. "I am frightened by what is happening," said Major Owens, an 11-term Democratic Congressman from New York and a leading member of the Congressional Black Caucus. "Our party is in grave danger. This Republican movement is going to expand exponentially unless we do something." At the time, Owens was right to be worried. Despite Bush's monumental Katrina bungle and the deep hatred of Bush and his policies by many blacks, his popularity was still in the range of the comprehensible.

❖ ❖ ❖ ❖ ❖

The Katrina disaster didn't change the other racially favorable demographic for the GOP: The Joint Center for Political and Economic Studies, a Washington, D.C., based black political research institute, found that between 2000 and 2004, the percent of blacks who registered as Democrats dropped 11 percent. One in three young blacks under age 35 said they were Independents. The percent of blacks registered as Republican tripled. The Republican bump-up and the Democratic slide among blacks had major political consequences.

The potential for energizing and mobilizing blacks for conservative political issues had markedly increased. The 2004 Joint Center for Political and Economic Studies 2004 National Opinion

Poll found that sixty percent of blacks supported school vouchers and half supported Social Security privatization.

Other polls showed that black evangelical and community-based groups favored Bush's faith-based initiative. Even though Bush's post-Katrina political support had frayed, Democratic pollster Ron Lester noted in a *Washington Post* interview in January 2005 that the black electorate is more religious and more conservative than the black population. According to Lester, nearly 80 percent of black voters identified themselves as churchgoers. That hadn't changed either. Those were black population demographics that caused Bush and the GOP to think that they could — no, *had* actually cracked the mono-lithic black vote. The number of black voters who backed the Republicans in the 2004 presidential election had nudged up their hopes even more.

A tepid black Democratic turnout, combined with the 13 percent of the black votes Bush received, helped him win Florida outright and avoid a repeat of the election debacle of 2000. Republican gains among blacks were even more dramatic in Ohio: Bush garnered nearly 20 percent of the black vote there. To put that in perspective, if Bush had gotten the same proportion of the black vote in the state as he did in 2000, his margin of victory over John Kerry would have narrowed from 118,000 votes to 25,000 votes. Given the large number of pro-visional ballots filed in Ohio, the Democrats almost certainly would have challenged the election certification. It would have been Florida 2000 all over again.

The GOP's gains among black voters were no accident. In August 2000, Rove told *Washington Post* national political writer Tom Edsall that the Republicans must reject "the use of such issues as affirmative action, and 'welfare queens' that past GOP candidates had employed in a calculated bid to polarize the electorate and put together a predominantly white majority." That also included renouncing all efforts to suppress the black vote. There was some evidence that the GOP operatives had done just that in some states, notably Florida, Missouri, and Ohio.

The GOP's new big-tent racial strategy translated into Bush's public pledge at the Republican convention in Philadelphia in August to make *diversity* and *inclusion* the new watchwords in the Republican Party. That wasn't hard. Blacks were virtually invisible at the Republican National Convention in San Diego in 1996. They constituted only 51 of the more than 2,000 delegates. TV stations seemed to go out of their way to stick a camera in the faces of the handful of black delegates during the televised portion of the proceedings. This created the badly distorted notion that blacks had a greater presence and played a bigger role at the convention than they actually did.

The much-publicized breakthrough that GOP convention officials claimed that they had made on the diversity front was far less than met the eye. Kay Cole James, a Virginia college professor, made history when she became the first black GOP convention secretary. In fierce behind-the-scenes maneuvering, though, James was denied the chair of the convention's abortion subcommittee. The convention committees and subcommittees made the crucial policy-making decision. Despite Bush's diversity pledge, the number of black delegates at Philadelphia had only marginally grown.

But numbers do count at conventions. Conventions aren't just giant, splashy, national media photo-op, glad-handing, and political back-stroking extravaganzas. They imprint the party's philosophy and policy goals in the public mind. If blacks are missing from the convention's table, then their agenda will be given short shrift. "The number of black delegates at a convention insures that more attention will be given to black interests and thus potentially more votes for that party," NAACP Washington Bureau Director Hilary Shelton, observed. "The Democrats in recent years have understood that. The Republicans are now figuring that out."

❖ ❖ ❖ ❖ ❖

The paltry number of blacks who identified with the GOP dramatically changed following Bush's 2004 re-election victory when Rove and Mehlman publicly announced their all-out effort to accelerate the black voter shift to the GOP. The Katrina outcry didn't fundamentally change their strategy. Mehlman, in fact, even managed to turn Katrina on its head and find a sliver of silver lining in it for the GOP. He picked a chapter meeting of the prestigious Waterbury, Connecticut, branch of the NAACP to spin his upbeat message: "I think any time there's a natural disaster, the people who have the least get hurt the most. The message that I'm delivering is a message of hope and opportunity."

Mehlman's plan was still to toss money around among black conservative and evangelical groups, urge the promotion of high-profile blacks to administration positions, and relentlessly pump their names and status to advocate business-friendly policies that appealed to the post-civil-rights generation of young, upwardly mobile blacks. Equally importantly, Bush and Mehlman would test the political winds in 2006 and selectively back a new wave of black GOP candidates for gubernatorial and senatorial seats in Ohio, Pennsylvania, Maryland, and Michigan.

This wasn't a novel or unique strategy: Reagan had pioneered the same strategy two decades earlier. Though he was relentlessly anti-big government, welfare, and affirmative action, he refined Nixon's Southern Strategy of code-word race-baiting to lock in the white Southern vote, and he unleashed open warfare against civil rights leaders. He scoured the country in a search for blacks to fill key administration posts. During his tenure in the 1980s, Reagan found and boosted conservatives such as Clarence Thomas, Clarence Pendleton, Allan Keyes, and Samuel Pierce for administration spots.

Reagan and the Republicans aimed to build on the entrenched social conservatism of many blacks and create a new black leadership that embraced moral and family values, market capitalism, personal initiative, and self-help and were staunch Republican loyalists. This black conservative leadership could challenge civil rights leaders and liberal Democrats on racial issues and even on their pet policy issues that ostensibly had nothing to with race (such as Bush's plan to partially privatize social security). When polls showed the plan lagging badly among whites, GOP strategists openly wooed blacks to back the plan. They argued that blacks put more into, and get less in return from, the current social security system because they die younger.

Many blacks hated Bush's plan — as did many whites, including some conservatives — and thought it was lousy economics and a threat to their old age security. Yet garnering broader black support for some of Bush's initiatives was still very much in the White House's thinking.

The GOP had another page in its old playbook for achieving that goal. Reagan and Nixon had courted high-profile blacks to pitch for the party on controversial policy issues. They included such notables as Jackie Robinson, Sammy Davis, Jr., and Ralph Abernathy. At times, they sounded every bit as conservative on some issues as white GOP conservatives. Then there was Martin Luther King, Jr., and the issue of affirmative action. Conservatives didn't just attack affirmative action in the 1980s and 1990s; they twisted, bent, and eventually repackaged the issue into a defense of the colorblind society. An important part of the repackage job was to embrace King. GOP leaders and black conservatives wrapped themselves in his cloak and boldly claimed his fight for racial justice was their fight too and that he was at heart a social conservative and if he were alive he'd be in agreement with many of the GOP's ideals.

King's apparent social conservatism wedged the political door open wider for Republicans to court the black evangelicals. Their spectacular emergence in 2004 as a potent political force was a boon to the GOP and a cause for concern among Democrats. The great untold story of campaign 2004 was that black evangelicals helped tip Ohio and the White House to Bush. If Republicans played their anti-gay-marriage and anti-abortion cards right, they'd get even more black evangelical votes in the 2006 national elections and the 2008 presidential election. The increase in the black vote remained the GOP's longed-for hope before Katrina struck and Bush's mild popularity bump-up among blacks went into a headlong tailspin.

Even before Katrina, the social conservatism of many blacks and their opposition to gay marriage didn't trigger a rush of black votes to Bush. The issue of jobs, the economy, health

care, and affirmative action trumped gay marriage among blacks
— and that included many black evangelicals. The GOP
dumped millions of faith-based dollars into the pockets of select
mega-church black ministers; wined and dined them at the
White House; and swayed to the gospel beat at their churches.
The polls still found that black Christians and their ministers
were also just as passionate in backing affirmative action and
more federal aid for jobs and education. The conservatism of
most black voters stretched no farther than family values beliefs.
That posed another dilemma for Republicans or, more partic-
ularly, for Bush.

Before, during, and after the Florida vote crisis in 2000 that
ignited bitter charges that Republicans connived to disenfran-
chise Florida blacks and grab the White House, black antipathy
toward Bush was burning, impassioned, and relentless. The
majority of black voters didn't just dislike his politics — they
disliked him. If Bush said the earth was round, many blacks
would say it's flat. Katrina and the Bennett quip simply reinforced their visceral disdain for him. Their contempt for him
exceeds their contempt for Reagan, and he worked especially
hard to earn the enmity of blacks with his assault on affirmative
action and open war with civil rights leaders. That visceral
dislike has dumbfounded Bush.

At a press conference in October 2005, he openly mused
that he'd done everything possible to win black support. He
cited his high-level appointments of Condoleezza Rice and
former Secretary of State Colin Powell as proof. The appointments of Rice, Powell and Rod Page (former Secretary of Education) broke new ground, but it did not impress blacks. They
were widely seen as political yes-men and -women for Bush's

hurtful policies. Rice's initial seeming public indifference to the Katrina debacle didn't help matters.

Bush's historic and abysmally low approval numbers among blacks in the October 2005 NBC–*Wall Street Journal* poll was flawed. Still, it was a huge warning sign that the GOP still had a long way to go before it could claim any significant allegiance from blacks.

To accomplish its goal of winning more black votes for Bush and for Republican candidates in state and local elections, Republicans would have to figure out (1) how to mesh the party's political conservatism with black's inherent social conservatism; (2) how to fight for a colorblind society, yet make racial appeals; (3) how to win more national elections in a nation whose majority in the next two decades will be non-white; (4) how to support, or better yet, cultivate more black candidates for state and national offices and not alienate its hard-core conservative base; and (5) how to make the Republican Party a moderate, racially diverse party.

A post-Bush GOP presidential candidate might well try to do that — indeed, almost certainly the next GOP presidential standard-bearer will have to do that, given that a major part of the electorate will be Hispanic, black, and increasingly Asian in 2008. The GOP's sworn political enemies would even welcome an effort to bag more minorities: "We're happy the Democratic Party may have to compete a little harder for votes," noted Shelton. "It may have taken (blacks) for granted the last several years."

The GOP's long relationship with black America has been one of court and scorn and sometimes both at the same time. That perplexing quandary still dogs the GOP in the 21st century. The GOP's challenge to itself and to black America is how to resolve that quandary. Before Katrina, Bush and Mehlman believed that they had a roaring chance to resolve it in the GOP's favor — to slice away at the Democratic stranglehold on the black vote and even to begin to build an emerging black GOP majority.

Bush and Mehlman were getting way ahead of themselves even at the time that they had begun to make headway on the racial front. The big majority of black voters still religiously voted Democratic, every member of the Congressional Black Caucus was a Democrat, and civil rights leaders were almost hysterically hostile to Bush. The NAACP, for instance, continued to hammer hard that Senate and House Republicans still were inherently hostile to greater funding for education, health care, job training, and to tighten employment discrimination measures. It gave nearly every Republican Senator and representative in the 2006 Congress an "F" grade on its legislative report card.

On the other hand, though the NAACP flunked Republicans in Congress and Democrats pounded Bush mercilessly on Katrina relief, it did not spell total doom for the GOP. The party had a bevy of high-profile, politically savvy blacks poised to make a serious run at senate, gubernatorial, and congressional seats in crucial battleground states. The list included Football Hall of Fame superstar Lynn Swann, Ohio Secretary of State Ken Blackwell, and popular black evangelist and co-chair of the Bush–Cheney 2004 African-American Campaign Committee Keith Butler in Michigan; Maryland Lieutenant Governor

Michael Steele; New York Secretary of State Randy Daniels; and Missouri State Representative Sherman Parker.

They were a formidable array of high-profile, politically connected black Republicans who could make a credible showing, if not win the races outright, and garner massive media attention. They took great pains to warn that they were not bait-and-switch GOP window dressing to con a few more blacks into the party but intended to be full players at the GOP table. Lynn Swann shouted to a nearly all-white gathering of GOP faithfuls at a Holiday Inn in Clarion, Pennsylvania, after announcing his gubernatorial intentions in 2006, "I'm not here to be the poster child for the Republican Party to say they're being inclusive by running an African-American." He was emphatic. "I'm here to win."

Whether they won or lost, it would still take much to build that emerging black GOP majority. The hard reality is that "Black folks distrust Republicans," noted Parker, "partially because they don't have a presence in the black community." Republicans hoped that Parker and the other black candidates would give them that sorely lacking visibility. NAACP Chairman Julian Bond, who has led a fierce charge against Bush policies every moment he's been in the White House, noted, "Republican policies have done more than anything to turn blacks against the party."

Nonetheless, Bush still held the key to unlocking the Democrats' grip on the black vote. In his December 2005 White House press conference, he promised to do a better job with African-Americans. If Bush keeps that promise, the GOP could snatch just enough battleground-state black support in future national elections to give it an edge over the Democrats. If he and the GOP didn't keep that promise, that — along with the monumental skepticism of the majority of blacks to GOP policies — would do much to ensure that the emerging black GOP majority would become the vanishing black GOP majority for years to come.

Chapter 2

The Other Reagan Revolution

I t was one of those rare moments that change the course of a person's life: When Ken Blackwell got an invitation to visit Ronald Reagan at the White House in the early 1980s, he was then suspended in a sort of political Never Never Land. The former Xavier University football star had made his mark in Cincinnati as the city's first black mayor in 1979.

At the time, Blackwell belonged to the Charterist Party, a nondescript political grouping. Although he considered himself more in line with centrist Democratic thinking on most issues, he was clearly searching for bigger things, and that could only be attained in and through the Democratic or Republican party. The Reagan meeting decided things for him. "I walked out of there knowing that I was going to join the party myself. It was clear to me that I stood a better chance of following my principles as a Republican."

It turned out to be a good decision for Blackwell and Republicans. He swept into office as Ohio Secretary of State and twice played a big role in helping bag Ohio for Bush and swinging the White House to Bush in 2004. In 2006, he had a good shot at being Ohio's first black governor. Then he'd be in an even better position to assure Republican dominance in the state in future elections. The prospect was not only a nightmare for Jesse Jackson, as Blackwell was fond of saying, but a nightmare for the Democrats. Blackwell's rise to the political heights, the GOP's courting of him, and the Reagan meeting were no accident.

The Reagan revolution is generally credited as one man's radical political vision to return America to a world in which God, patriotism, rugged individualism, anti-Communism, and family values ruled supreme. It was that. But there was another more discreet, less visible part of the Reagan revolution that flew way under the political radar of most at the time but would have profound political repercussions in the years to come. Blackwell was that visible example of Reagan's "other" revolution at work. That other revolution was to woo and cultivate young blacks to march in ideological lockstep with the GOP and be a counterforce to black Democrats and civil rights leaders.

❖   ❖   ❖   ❖   ❖

Reagan's novel racial offensive began not in Washington but in San Francisco in December 1980. For two days, more than one hundred delegates had gathered at what was ambitiously and boldly billed as "The Black Alternatives Conference." They were black scholars, activists, professionals, attorneys, doctors, journalists, and businesspersons. Most, but not all, were conservatives. Charles Hamilton and Percy Sutton were perfect examples of the political diversity of the conference participants. Hamilton rose to public fame and acclaim as coauthor of the seminal work on Black Power with 1960s black-power militant Stokely Carmichael. Sutton was a businessman, New York Democratic Party power broker, and legal advisor and long time supporter, friend, and confidant of Malcolm X. However, Hamilton and Sutton believed, as did the other conference participants, that government programs had failed the black poor, and the Democrats practiced plantation politics in taking the black vote for granted. The conference sought a political alternative to the tattered domestic and social policies of the Democrats.

The conference was the brainchild of Thomas Sowell, the iconoclastic black polemicist and scholar, and was bankrolled by the Institute for Contemporary Studies. Two former aides to then-California governor Ronald Reagan founded the Institute after Reagan was out of office in 1976.

The conference participants wasted no time in blasting welfare, entitlement programs, minimum wage laws, rent control, top-heavy government regulations, and affirmative action. They claimed that these programs had done monumental harm to the black poor. It increased their dependence on government and killed personal initiative. The only winners from the Democrats' welfare state policies were a relatively small, privileged group of black professionals and businesspersons. Sowell opened the conference by declaring it "a historic opportunity" and declared that black advancement was still the "great unfinished task" of the civil rights movement. He and the others were firmly convinced that their approach to social policy would have a profound

impact on race and black politics and that the published conference papers would be a "historic document."

This was not hyperbole from a few contrarian, alienated,
bitter academics or self-seeking political activists. Their ideas were
grounded in the social conservatism of towering black figures
such as Frederick Douglass, Booker T. Washington, W. E. B.
DuBois, and Marcus Garvey, as well as pioneer black conservatives Kelly Miller, George Schyuler, Manning Johnson, and a
core of older-generation black Republicans, such as President
Eisenhower's special assistant Frederick R. Morrow and Nixon's
assistant Arthur Fletcher. The themes of self-help, personal initiative, business development, and political diversity had been
recycled continuously over the past century. Civil rights leaders
had ridiculed and reviled black conservatives in the past, but
they had often embraced some of those same themes.

Jesse Jackson's Operation Push, the Southern Christian
Leadership Conference, and the NAACP were unabashed advocates of black economic self-sufficiency side-by-side with political activism. With the demise of civil rights street activism of the
1960's, these groups had grown increasingly more dependent
on major corporations to keep their doors open.

❖　❖　❖　❖　❖

By the mid-1980s, there were two major shifts in the
political and economic climate of America that virtually ensured
that black conservatives could no longer be marginalized and
ignored as they had been in past years. The first was the victory
of Reagan. Conservatives inched closer than ever to becoming
the dominant political force in America. They could now fund,
promote, and appoint blacks who shared their conservative views
to key political and policy-making positions.

The second was the changing face of black America. This fueled the quiet revolution in conservative thinking among the new crop of black leaders. While many blacks had lost ground, due in part to conservative economic policies, many blacks had also gained ground, due in part to those same conservative business-friendly growth policies and the residue of social spending programs. In the 1960s, federal entitlement programs, civil rights legislation, equal opportunity statutes, and affirmative action programs initiated during Lyndon Johnson's administration broke the last barriers of legal segregation. The path to universities and corporations for some blacks was now wide open. More blacks than ever did what their parents only dreamed of: They fled big-city blighted inner-city areas in Chicago, New York, Los Angeles, Detroit, and Atlanta in droves.

During the 1970s, more than 2 million more blacks were employed, and the number of blacks in the workforce climbed to an all-time high. By 1980, young blacks aged 25-34 had narrowed the income gap with white males to 85 percent. In 1970, one in seven black families had incomes over $35,000. A decade later the proportion had dropped to one in five. The percent of black families with incomes over $50,000 nearly doubled during the 1970s.

The administration of President Jimmy Carter did much to boost the expansion of the black middle class. It strengthened federal programs that radically boosted the number of and money allocated for grants, loans, and technical training for minority businesses. More black businesspersons now had the means and the expertise to expand from the traditional small-time mom-and-pop grocery stores and service businesses into petroleum and energy, manufacturing, automotive sales, investments, and equity trading. That helped create a moderate and conservative black business class that had a vested interest in lower taxes, fewer government regulations, and strengthening ties to corporate America. The era and the need for protest among wide segments of the black middle class had abruptly ended.

Many in the new and expanded black middle class were upwardly mobile, career-oriented, college-educated, professional businesspersons and academics, and they plainly flourished economically. By the end of the Reagan years of the 1980s, an estimated one in ten blacks was affluent enough to move to the suburbs. The expansion of tract homes, condos, and apartments made their move easier. In the 1990s, the stampede of black business and professional people from these areas accelerated. Much of black wealth, as with white wealth, was now concentrated in fewer hands. Great Society programs, relatively low unemployment, the passage of civil rights laws, the continued migration of blacks from farms to industrial jobs, and the collapse of racial barriers in corporations powered the black middle class's growth.

The post-civil-rights generation of blacks was a decade removed from the civil rights battles of the 1960s. They were not doused by water hoses, forced to use Jim Crow water fountains, and bitten by snarling police dogs. They had not seen or experienced the naked and brutal face of Southern segregation.

Black conservatives gave the credit for their success to Reagan. That was not completely a self-serving exaggeration; more blacks were employed, had graduated from high school and college, were employed in the professions, had climbed into the ranks of corporate management, and owned their own businesses at the end of Reagan's time in office than at the beginning of it.

❖ ❖ ❖ ❖ ❖

But that told only one part of Black America's story. While the black middle class became more numerous and more prosperous, the black poor also became larger — but poorer. The estimate was that one out of three blacks earned an income below the federal poverty limit, and most had almost no access to quality health care, lived in poor, crime- and gang-plagued neighborhoods, and their children went to mostly segregated, underserved public schools.

The class rift between the black *haves* and *have-nots* began inching wider and wider. In the 1950s, sociologist E. Franklin Frazier warned that many blacks were becoming what he scornfully branded a black bourgeoisie that controlled the wealth and power within the black community and that had turned their backs on their own people. In Frazier's view, the black bourgeoisie had begun to ape the values, standards, and ideals of the white middle class and to distance themselves from the black poor. Decades later, before he made his break with conservatives, black academic Glenn Loury saw the same class schisms among blacks that Frazier bemoaned: "There is a growing divergence in the social and economic experiences of black Americans."

Loury, as Frazier before him, greatly overstated the class cleavage among blacks. There were many blacks who self-identified as the part of the black middle class who were only one paycheck, one lay-off, or one firing or job outsourcing from impoverishment. They too were subject to racial discrimination in far too many cases. It was indisputable, though, that many black professionals had prospered and were repelled by the high crime, violence, and family absenteeism among some in poor, black, inner-city neighborhoods.

The climb of the black middle class to loftier economic heights and the slide of the black poor further toward the bottom of the economic ladder had a profound effect on mainstream civil-rights organizations. The traditional civil rights organizations — the NAACP, SCLC, SNCC, and CORE — were defunct, in decline, or had radically redefined their agenda. The fight for affirmative action, economic parity, professional advancement, and expanding black business replaced 1) fighting poverty and unemployment; 2) improving grossly underserved, under-performing, failing inner city schools; 3) self-help; 4) family stability; and 5) battling crime, drugs, and gang violence. They had seemingly shifted the public goal of "all" blacks, including the black poor.

That agenda did nothing to address the plight of the black poor. Nevertheless, it gave black conservatives and the participants at the Fairmont Conference the ideological and political weapon they needed to hammer mainstream civil rights leaders for ignoring the black poor. They had found the broad and tender Achilles heel of civil rights organizations, and they aimed their political arrows at it every chance they got.

In a wrap-up statement at the close of the conference, Sowell threw down the gauntlet: "The issue is not that the government gives too much help to the poor. The problem is that government creates too much harm for the poor." That statement was more than a (disputed) fact. It once again opened wide the age-old debate over liberalism versus conservatism, big government versus shrunken government, and entitlement programs and welfare versus a free-market economy (minus government regulations). Having the finger pointed at civil rights leaders for failing the black poor was a boon to the black conservatives and ultimately the GOP. The welfare state proponents were liberal Democrats, and black conservatives never tired of pointing that out.

Reagan eagerly pounded on that theme.

With the popularity of his administration growing in the mid-1980s, it was now respectable to be black and conservative. For the first time in American history, black conservatives had political and media cachet and name recognition. They were quoted, feted, wined, and dined, and their ideas were widely debated and discussed by everyone in the media and on Capitol Hill — and even by civil rights leaders.

A wide-eyed Clarence Thomas, then an obscure Missouri assistant attorney general, suddenly found himself a hot ticket item when he came back from the San Francisco conference. "After we got back from the Fairmont Conference, it was the first time I had any kind of articles written about me. All of a sudden, my views are in a major paper — the *Washington Post*." Reagan officials moved quickly to exploit the political potential of the new crop of black conservatives — such as Thomas — for the GOP.

He had little choice but to hunt for men such as Thomas. As long as white conservative males were the point men for his administration's attack on civil rights and affirmative action, Reagan was vulnerable to the charge that he was a racist. Republicans had to change that. Reagan now could draw on a core of reliable, black, conservative activists who were philosophically and politically attuned to his administration's polices. But even if he had felt no need to find blacks to loyally defend his policies, he still would have had to make black appointments. Every

Republican president in the modern era had followed that practice. It was a matter of principle and pragmatism.

Reagan put heat on White House personnel director Pendleton James to step up black recruitment efforts. James got the message and issued a directive to his staff, bluntly demanding, "Quit bringing in all these white guys."

The problem was not that Reagan officials actively discouraged blacks, but that the blacks they approached as potential hires flatly said no. The depth of hatred of Reagan and his policies was so great among civil rights leaders and a large number of blacks that any identification with Reagan was a political, and maybe personal, kiss of death.

But it was Reagan's opposition to affirmative action that had raised the ire of civil rights leaders to a white-hot level. They stepped up their ideological attack on the major premise of the black conservatives, namely that affirmative action programs did not alleviate the plight of the black poor. They dismissed it as a false, self-serving argument black conservatives used to torpedo affirmative action. It was valid — up to a point. But it begged the question: Did affirmative action programs primarily benefit black businesspersons and professionals and do nothing for the black poor? That was the cornerstone argument of the black conservatives, and they came back to that theme time and again during the Reagan years. Blacks in America's inner cities were poorer, more numerous, and more desperate. Yet, at the same time, the work force did grow and more blacks were able to get into college and enter into the professional fields.

In that sense, it was a victory for affirmative action. Those among the black poor who bettered their condition benefited from affirmative action along with the black professionals. But affirmative action was hardly the sole reason for their economic bump up. It was also due to the economic expansion in some sectors of the economy and in part to the decrease in discrimination in some industries that felt pressure to hire more blacks and minorities. Blacks — including the less skilled and even some of the poor — would have made gains even if affirmative action programs had never existed. Conservatives could rightly claim that the programs worked unevenly among blacks. And civil rights leaders could also claim that all blacks benefited from them. But if the black poor did not benefit from affirmative action, what was the alternative? Conservatives did not routinely demand that affirmative action programs be expanded to include lower-income blacks *or* whites.

This was a troubling issue for black conservatives. They had to address it to avoid the charge that they were insensitive to blacks and bought and paid-for hatchet men for Reagan officials.

Shelby Steele recognized the soft spot. He burst on the scene in the early 1980s with his prize-winning book, *The Content of Character: A New Vision of Race in America*. It was a sharp, bare-your-chest, personal polemic against affirmative action and entitlement programs. He quickly became a fixture on the talk show circuit battling liberal Democrats and civil rights leaders on racial issues. Steele rhetorically asked the question, If not affirmative action, then what? His answer was to give "disadvantaged children" better schools, job training, safer neighborhoods, and more financial aid for college.

Steele did not elaborate on the means to bring that about. At the very least, it required probably more not less government funding and the expansion of entitlement programs. That flew in the face of black conservative's and Steele's emphasis on personal initiative and self-help as the keys to black advancement. In any case, Steele dropped his "then what" at the end of his chapter on affirmative action, and it looked and felt like more of an afterthought than an alternative blueprint to affirmative action.

The obvious alternative was to aggressively push corporations to expand job and training programs and remedial education, increase tax breaks and incentives for inner city business training and investment, and establish and increase support for empowerment zones. But few conservatives had the stomach to wage a sustained battle in Congress for those programs or to kick at the shins of big corporations to prod them to do more to hire and promote minorities.

Still, Steele's emergence as a conservative media star firmly established that there was a rising core of recognizable, energetic, conservative blacks willing to push the GOP on its core issues. They quickly became even more widely quoted and hailed as policy-making and media players. Their emergence gave a strong hint that there was a growing number of blacks who had reservations about affirmative action.

Opinion polls in the mid-1970s found a firm consensus among blacks and whites that racial discrimination was still a fact of life in America and that government agencies should do everything to eliminate it. When they were asked if the government should provide jobs and special programs for blacks in order to end discrimination, the majority of whites said no. By the early 1980s, there was a surprise: A 1981 CBS–*New York Times* poll asked, "Because of past discrimination, blacks who need it *(should/should not)* get some help from the government that white people in similar economic circumstances don't get."

A decisive majority of blacks agreed that blacks should not get the assistance at the expense of the poor whites. Three years later a Gallup poll asked a similar question. While slightly more than 25 percent of blacks said that blacks should get preferential treatment in hiring, more than 60 percent said that hiring and promotions should be based on ability. A CBS–*New York Times* poll in 1985 asked, "Where there has been job discrimination, should preference in hiring or promotion be given to women and minorities?"

Nearly fifty percent of blacks said they opposed racial preferences. Civil rights leaders dismissed the poll findings as skewed, flawed, biased, and not giving an accurate gauge of black sentiment. The great majority of blacks backed some form of affirmative action, and their barrage of discrimination lawsuits, countless protests, and demonstrations against corporate discrimination made the results appear false. They weren't totally false. The Protestant ethic of hard work, personal responsibility, and initiative is deeply ingrained in American beliefs. Success and merit are intimately connected, and one can't be attained without the other. It was precisely that strong work ethic among blacks in the nightmare years of Jim Crow segregation laws and in the immediate post-civil-rights-era years that gave them the incentive to hurdle the obstacles of discrimination and achieve success.

Affirmative action seemed to run counter to that work ethic. It fueled suspicions among whites and defensiveness among blacks to the implication that they could not compete without special programs. That permanently imprinted blacks with the scarlet letter of failure. In a darker context, it reinforced the racist notion of black inferiority. Sowell repeatedly stressed that point in his landmark 1984 book *Civil Rights: Rhetoric or Reality:*

"Pride of achievement is also undermined by the civil rights vision that assumes credit for minority achievement. This makes minority achievement suspect in their own eyes and in the eyes of the larger society." It shouldn't have made it suspect. In the majority of cases, blacks advanced up the corporate ladder not because of affirmative action but because of their education, talent, energy, and desire. Even so, that did nothing to allay white suspicions and protests that the blacks had moved up exclusively because of their color.

In the tumultuous wars that raged over affirmative action in the mid 1990s on American college and university campuses, that argument became the reason often cited for dumping or radically altering affirmative action programs. To ward off accusations that blacks couldn't make it without a hand up or a handout, some black educators made the same argument. That didn't quiet the debate, and it didn't end the attacks on affirmative action programs.

❖ ❖ ❖ ❖ ❖

Black conservative writers and academics — such as Steele and Sowell — were too erudite, too cloistered, and too far removed from the thick of the political action in Washington to affect policy change. The tricky task was to find black conservatives who could articulate conservative principles — in short, a fresh face who did not carry any political baggage. It didn't take Reagan long to find that person.

Clarence Thomas was a dream match for Reagan. His impoverished, pull-yourself-up-by-your-bootstraps rise from the harshly segregated backwash hamlet of Pin Point, Georgia, and his conversion from campus radical to conservative ideologue fit perfectly into Reagan's free-market, shun-government-entitle-ment-programs philosophy. He did not have the baggage that HUD Secretary Samuel Pierce and Clarence Pendleton had. Pierce was hit with allegations of corruption and influence peddling. And Pendleton made news as the first African-American to head the U.S. Civil Rights Commission in 1982. However, Pendleton's shoot-from-the-lip attacks on civil rights leaders and his shady business dealings kept him in perennial hot water with both the commission and the Democrats. He was a political embar-rassment. Neither Pierce nor Pendleton could mantle the Repub-lican party with the veneer of respectability that Reagan needed to sell his policies to conservative leaning blacks. Thomas had real possibilities.

The crisp attacks on civil rights laws, affirmative action, and government entitlement programs that were made at the Fair-mont Conference had energized him. Thomas hoped that Sowell could put together a permanent organization to advance conserv-ative programs among blacks. That didn't happen. But as a result of a profile the *Washington Post* did on him at the conference, he came to Reagan's attention. That started Thomas's decade-long odyssey from lower-level Reagan administration functionary to the U.S. Supreme Court. During that trek, Thomas came to sym-bolize political evil incarnate to civil rights leaders and black Democrats. To conservatives he stood tall as the man who's will-ing to pit himself against liberal racial orthodoxy, defy the civil rights establishment, and uphold principled conservatism.

Thomas is also the lighting rod in the debate over whether blacks who embrace conservatism are pawns of the GOP or whether they instead represent a legitimate and deep political and social trend in black communities. That debate posed the deeper dilemma of just how independent could blacks, even black conservatives, be as administration appointees and remain safely within the bounds of conservative orthodoxy and in the good graces of the GOP? Resolution of that question would depend on the time, place, and issues involved.

Thomas confronted that dilemma in his early days in the 1980s as chair of the EEOC (Equal Employment Opportunity Commission). He was expected to aggressively push Reagan administration policies on the commission, and that meant a frontal attack on affirmative action programs. In the beginning he did not see himself as a GOP hit man against affirmative action programs and employment discrimination regulations. The issue came to a head when Thomas had to decide how the commission would deal with an affirmative action hiring and promotion lawsuit brought by black officers against the New Orleans police department. In December 1982 — a scant few months after Thomas took over the reins at the EEOC — a federal court panel finally approved a settlement. The city agreed to hire or promote one black officer for every white officer hired or promoted until the department reached parity. Reagan officials hit the roof, and screamed reverse discrimination. But Thomas initially agreed with the affirmative action plan, and so did a group of black Republicans.

These Republicans told Reagan that his political strategies had caused "self-inflicted damage with black voters." The Republicans were both moderates and conservatives, and for the most part they believed that Reagan's economic policies benefited blacks. Though Thomas was not at the meeting, he agreed with them. He argued that to overturn the settlement would "invalidate innumerable conciliation agreements, consent decrees, and adjudicated decrees to which the commission had been a party."

Reagan officials got wind of it, and Thomas was squarely on the hot seat. Attorney General William Smith French sent a stern message that there was no room on the Reagan team for dissenters: "The Reagan administration must speak with one voice." That message was firmly reiterated to Thomas in a meeting at the White House. The federal court eventually turned Reagan down, and the settlement stood.

Thomas was an administration appointee, and a high-profile one at that. Politics and ideology trumped any personal or political differences he had with the administration over policy. It would have been the same if a Democratic official tried to buck the established policy set by his or her boss if that boss were a Democratic president. Thomas's knuckling under also proved the larger point that no matter what a political appointee's ideology is — liberal or conservative — when they're in an administration, for the most part, they are captive to the administration's dictates.

Some top black presidential appointees before and after Thomas — Fred Morrow, Arthur Fletcher, and Colin Powell — as they served respectfully in the Eisenhower, Nixon, and Bush, Jr., administrations, occasionally bucked their bosses and took maverick positions on issues, and it didn't cost them their jobs or compromise their core moderate or conservative political beliefs. However, on key issues and policy questions they toed the party and administration line. If they hadn't, they wouldn't have lasted in their positions.

The strict adherence to conservative GOP policies by Thomas and some of the other Fairmont conference participants was the tonic the party needed to counter the liberal arguments on the vital policy issues of welfare, affirmative action, and government entitlements. They were not kooks, quacks, or aberrations. They merely reflected the thinking of a growing segment of upwardly mobile, career-oriented blacks of the post-civil rights era.

They also forced the GOP, civil rights leaders, and the Democrats to confront complex questions that defied easy, formula answers on race and the limits of liberalism, conservatism, and federal power. By the end of the Reagan years, they sparked a probing challenge on a number of such important racial and political topics as the relevance of affirmative action, the civil rights leadership's agenda for the black poor, the benefit to the poor of welfare and government spending, and the Democrats' penchant for taking the black vote for granted. They also challenged white conservatives to share power with black conservatives and that included first and foremost major decision-making power. The lack of any significant number of blacks at the 1980 and 1984 Republican presidential conventions seemed to show that the party's practice on racial inclusion lagged badly behind its rhetoric about it.

The final challenge to white conservatives was whether they could truly accept blacks as conservatives. That question nagged Thomas even before his rise to national prominence. In June 1987, he confronted it head-on in a speech at the Heritage Foundation. Thomas lashed out at the notion that black conservatives must be purer in their conservatism than whites to be considered legitimate conservatives and therefore accepted: "For blacks the litmus test was fairly clear. You must be against affirmative action and against welfare. And your opposition had to be adamant and constant or you would be suspected of being a closet liberal."

Thomas relentlessly contended that blacks had a right to be conservative and that did not make them sellouts or Uncle Toms. In choosing to embrace conservatism and defend Reagan administration policies — and later in his take-no-prisoners rulings and opinions on the Supreme Court — Thomas shattered the notion that blacks must and do think, act, and march in unison with each other on all racial issues. This was racist, patronizing, narrow, and ultimately self-defeating.

Yet Sowell, Thomas, Pendleton, and Steele would not have risen to notoriety in the 1980s if the GOP had not needed them as much as they needed the GOP. Their match was more than a marriage of convenience: It was a pact born of political necessity. That political necessity would have proven illusory if not for a rapidly expanding and prospering black middle class. Reagan's policies provided a greater number of blacks with more jobs, education, higher wages, and a better standard of living than they had ever had in America. That success came without increased welfare and government entitlement programs or more civil rights laws.

Even though the poor grew more numerous and were shoved further toward the economic margins, conservatives had it both ways. They used that fact as another way to shellac the liberal social and economic policies of the Democrats, even though some of those policies provided a safety net for many of the poor. In the end, the stock of black conservatives rose.

Reagan and GOP officials had groomed and nurtured them. Now they gave them the rationale that they needed to sell the GOP to black America and at the same time fend off charges that the party was racist. Black conservatives had to prove that they could provide a genuine leadership alternative to that of mainstream civil rights groups. The challenge posed for them would set the tone for the political debate for the next two decades over what the best Right political course should be for black Americans and who should guide that course. The credit and blame for igniting that debate went to Reagan.

Civil rights leaders tagged the Reagan presidency the single worst period for racial progress in recent U.S. history. Much of the focus on Reagan and his relations with blacks concentrates almost exclusively on the rancor between his administration and civil rights leaders. But Reagan set in motion a countertrend in black leadership: The new, young, black conservative thinkers and political activists had put a black face on GOP policies. They could spin, prime, and defend its policies on affirmative action, welfare, laissez faire capitalism, and anti-government regulations with the best of white conservatives. Bush's controversial federal court appeals nominee, black California Supreme Court Justice Janice Rogers Brown, once brashly claimed that she was "one of the few conservatives left in America."

Best of all, they could challenge the legitimacy of civil rights leaders and black Democrats to be the sole voice of black America. While the vast majority of blacks then and now have not — and will not — break ranks with the Democrats, there are more than enough who already have. And there are more than a few who are more than willing to proudly embrace conservatism.

That was Reagan's other revolution. In an interview before the start of his gubernatorial campaign, Ken Blackwell reminded the world of it: "I am a natural heir of the Reagan revolution."

Chapter 3

Judging Clarence Thomas

There were warm smiles, tears of joy and appreciation, and a wave of nostalgia within the throng gathered at the home of black conservative pundit Armstrong Williams in January 2005. The guests were there for a breakfast reception and to receive rewards for their pioneer achievements in the cause of black conservatism. During the informal ceremonies, each received a commemorative coin honoring Crispus Attucks, the black man who was the first casualty of the American Revolutionary War. The honorees had all served in the administrations of Republican presidents Nixon, Ford, and Reagan.

They had racked up many firsts in their appointments to posts in the Labor Department, Office of Minority Business Affairs, and the Agency for International Development. They had been administrators, directors, and deputy directors in their departments. Williams praised them for their skill, expertise, and achievement in running major governmental departments. He took special note that blacks did and could serve in key policy-making positions within Republican administrations and that Republican Presidents were more than willing to appoint them to those positions even when Democrats didn't.

The appointees had been derided and ostracized by civil rights leaders for their conservative views and for serving in Republican administrations, but the appointees held firm to their views. Williams gushed, "These are the people who are the architects and builders of the black conservative movement." John Wilkes, who served as Nixon's deputy labor secretary, recalled how, in those days, "nobody wanted to deal with us."

They bemoaned the fact that being black, conservative, and Republican in 2005 was no longer a novelty. Black Republicans were, mused Ford appointee Leonora Alexander, no longer "a close-knit group." That was the great triumph for black conservatism.

The black conservatives who gathered at Williams's home were survivors. They had endured the scorn and abuse heaped on them by civil rights leaders. They had proven that blacks could be black and conservative and that they could readily make a credible case for their beliefs. In spite of their effort, the majority of blacks still regarded Republican policies as anti-poor, anti-black, and mean-spirited. And without the largesse of well-heeled conservative groups, the GOP — and even the presidents who employed the black men and women who gathered at Williams's home — would never have attained the prominence and visibility that they did.

Williams, for instance, was a talk-show host and a much sought-after media pundit on Republican positions concerning racial issues. As such, his conservative star had skyrocketed. A few days after the conservatives gathered at his place, he was embarrassed and reviled for grabbing nearly a quarter of a million dollars from the White House to pump Bush's education policies, all the while masquerading as a neutral media commentator. Yet, even after the scandal broke and Williams was bounced from his spot as a commentator on a few media outlets, he was still a frequent guest on talk shows defending conservative policies.

Despite the strides the aging gathering of black conservatives had made in getting their message out and the party support they enjoyed, it would take more than fond memories, nostalgia, and pride to convince more blacks that Republicans weren't their enemies. That remained the tormenting challenge for black conservatives and the GOP.

Thomas wasn't at Williams's soiree. Yet far more than anyone who was there, his career has typified the hard row that pioneer black conservatives had to hoe to make being black and conservative respectable or even desirable. He is the quintessential standard by which many blacks judge the GOP and conservatism. It has been that way during the more-than quarter century Thomas has been in the media and public limelight. It's crucial to examine the ins and outs of his Republican years to understand why that is, and the influence that he's had in shaping the GOP's promotion and handling of other conservative blacks during the 1990s and the present.

Thomas is savaged or praised for his views and opinions from all sides. Civil rights leaders pound him as a black man who betrayed his race. His defenders hail him as a black man who is independent enough to think for himself and defy racial pigeonholing. Whether he's back-patted or name-called, race has always lurked close to the surface — often too close for the thin-skinned Thomas. The one issue above all others that marks Thomas as the puppet whose string is continually pulled by white conservative puppeteers is his close alignment on the court with fellow Supreme Court jurist Antonin Scalia.

Scalia supposedly does the thinking, writes the opinions, and provides the political and judicial philosophy they share, and Thomas obediently follows along.

Thomas and Scalia have voted in agreement more than 90 percent of the time on legal issues. That high percentage of agreement reinforced the notion that Thomas is a big, dumb black man who can't make legal move on his own without approval from his white mentor. While Thomas takes blazing heat from civil rights leaders for conservative rulings on affirmative action, the death penalty, prisoner rights, school vouchers, and abortion, Scalia mostly gets a Teflon pass from them.

Before his departure from the high court bench, Thurgood Marshall warned Thomas that he would be held to a far harsher standard of scrutiny on and away from the bench than white conservatives in the same position. And Marshall's was the diametrically opposite view from Thomas's, both legally and politically. Thomas got the warning during a two-hour talk with the pioneer civil rights fighter shortly before his own confirmation war in October 1991.

The double standard Marshall warned of was especially glaring in that there there has been no criticism of the close relationship Marshall had with his counterpart, William Brennan. They marched in virtual lockstep during their days on the court in both their opinions and casting votes on crucial cases. In fact, they voted more alike in an even higher percentage of cases than have Thomas and Scalia. Marshall deferred to Brennan in intracourt negotiations with the other judges before important votes were taken. Marshall and the other judges regarded Brennan as the court's consensus builder. Marshall and Brennan's clerks constantly discussed cases, compared notes, and drafted opinions that they knew both men agreed on.

Marshall was black and liberal. Brennan was white and liberal. Civil rights and civil liberties groups lionized them both. It was natural, even expected, that two justices who shared the same judicial and political philosophy would work together. When Thomas and Scalia worked together, Thomas immediately became his lackey. There was not a peep of criticism that Marshall was Brennan's judicial twin, let alone that he took orders from him.

Thomas's conservative, unorthodox, and often far beyond the legal pale opinions on these issues were well known by the time he hit the court in 1991. There was rarely a surprise in his opinions or his votes, but at times, he cast the lone dissenting vote in cases concerning the death penalty, discrimination, age bias, first amendment, and foreign prisoner rights.

On a deeper level, the charge that he is Scalia's pet terrier is the euphemistic way of saying that blacks are puppets and Republicans are the string pullers. Thomas chose the occasion of the National Bar Association banquet in Memphis in 1998 to refute the charge. Thomas mixed sarcasm with anger when he bellowed to the black law group that Scalia was not his Pied Piper on the court and that if he dared think differently "someone must be putting these strange ideas into my head and my opinions."

In his cautious first public appearance in May 1993 after his bruising court confirmation battle, he spoke to a friendly audience at Mercer University, a conservative law school in Georgia. He cloaked himself in the martyr's garment and said that he expected to be treated badly among blacks for challenging liberal opinion: "As a black person straying from the tenets of (racial) orthodoxy ... you were [considered] a traitor to your race. [To them] you were not a real black, and you were forced to pay for your ideological trespass." Civil rights groups have done everything they could to make Thomas pay — and pay dearly — for his racial apostasy.

Yet no matter how outlandish and obstructionist his votes on the court might appear, Thomas has marched in lockstep with the political conservatism of many whites and the social conservatism of many blacks. Three years after he bared his soul on the racial hurt he felt Anita Hill and other liberals inflicted on him, he was invited to speak to black parents and students at a middle school in Landover, Maryland.

It seemed innocent enough. It was the sort of function that public figures are routinely invited to. Because the invitee was Thomas, that made it anything but routine. The local NAACP objected. The school board bowed to the pressure and uninvited Thomas. That might have been the end of it except that many of the black parents and students were outraged. They demanded that Thomas be allowed to speak, although not because they embraced his politics or him.

It was first and foremost an issue of free speech. One group should not have the right to dictate who could or couldn't speak. It was also tacit recognition that while many black parents disagreed with his views, he still had a right to those views, and they wanted to hear him state them if for no other reason than to challenge them. Thomas eventually spoke, and some parents and students did demonstrate against him. His appearance and talk were a significant victory — and not solely for Thomas. It was a testament to the maturity of the blacks who were willing to listen to him. They would make their own decisions about Thomas and his views without being censored by his black critics, even if many in the audience vehemently detested his politics, his Bush ties, and even him.

The parents and students won that battle. That made civil rights leaders even more determined to publicly silence Thomas. They didn't have long to wait. A few months later, word was leaked that Thomas would speak at a youth banquet in Maryland. The Maryland and Delaware chapters of the NAACP swung into action. They called him "divisive and polarizing" and demanded that the invitation be withdrawn. They threatened demonstrations. Thomas tactfully withdrew. It was not a political event; it was a charity function. The NAACP's forced action was more divisive and polarizing than Thomas's appearance. There was no mention of what the parents, sponsors, banquet organizers, or youth themselves thought of an outside group dictating who could or couldn't speak, let alone what they thought of the speaker's views. It didn't matter. The NAACP chapter had won their victory — this time.

❖   ❖   ❖   ❖   ❖

Thomas remained the hard symbol to civil rights groups of everything wrong with the courts and, as they saw it, the bankruptcy of black conservatism. That issue came crashing to a head at the same NBA convention where Thomas spoke in July 1998. Seven years earlier the organization had split down the middle over whether or not to endorse Thomas for the high court. The sores hadn't healed. The invitation to speak was made by the chair of the group's judicial council. By now it had become a ritual. When Thomas got an invitation to speak, the anti-Thomas forces quickly mobilized to try and stop him.

Some members immediately demanded that the invitation be withdrawn. Harvard Law Professor Leon Higginbotham, Jr., a former U.S. Appeals Court judge and a civil rights icon in his own right, had railed against Thomas for years. He rallied the opposition to the speech. If they proved unsuccessful in stopping Thomas from speaking, the protesters planned to hold a counter-workshop on civil rights during his speech.

In demanding that Thomas be uninvited, Higginbotham argued, "By the very nature of your invitation, you give Thomas an imprimatur that he has never had from any responsible organization within the African-American community." It was a curious argument. Higginbotham conveniently forgot, ignored, or deliberately dismissed the support Thomas got during his Supreme Court confirmation battle from the SCLC (Southern Christian Leadership Conference), the Urban League, many members of the NBA, and thousands of black citizens, as well as the numerous invitations he received from other black groups to speak during his years on the court. That didn't count. The aim was to demonize Thomas and those blacks who dared extend their support to him or interest in him.

The association stood firm and refused to withdraw the invitation. Higginbotham's counterpart on the appeals court, Damon Keith, who did not share Thomas's opinions and views, edged closer to the real importance of why Thomas should be allowed to speak: "We aren't going to be bullied and intimidated by a few people." To disagree with Thomas was legitimate. However, to censor his views was not. Keith rightfully would have none of it.

In his speech, Thomas poured out the accumulated rage and frustration from the years of abuse heaped on him. He raged that not only was he being held to a higher standard by other blacks, but that blacks who were conservative were not even entitled to have their views. Whites could be conservative but blacks couldn't be: "Somehow we have come to exalt the new black stereotype above all and demand conformity to that norm."

The applause was polite and reserved. Thomas probably made few converts. However, he rightly fingered the personal and political double standard that civil rights groups applied to him. White conservatives were praised, feted, and courted. During the Reagan years, they rose to become a dominant political force in American politics. Many blacks debated them and challenged their views in print, on TV, and in a wide range of other public venues; they didn't personally savage, name-call, and engage in rampant character assassination of them. They did all that and more to Thomas. The personal insults and attacks against him were repellent and repulsive and strayed way past the political fitness of his views and opinions, which was — or ought to be — the only standard used to commend or condemn a public figure. However, there was a reason so many blacks confused political criticism with character assassination.

Many blacks expect whites to espouse conservative views. That expectation is often colored by race. They cannot separate racism from conservatism. Since many blacks view whites as racists or of having racist views, they believe that their conservatism must be an expression of their racism. That racism and conservatism can be mutually incompatible is not considered; that requires making fine political and ideological distinctions apart from race. It is faulty, illogical, and wrong-headed, and many conservatives have been just as outspoken against racist ideas and practices as liberals. There is no one-to-one correlation between a conservative's espousal of free-market economics and their attack on government regulations and the championing of religious freedom and racial bigotry. Yet, the notion that a conservative is by definition a racist is deeply ingrained.

Republicans have no one but themselves to blame for this perception. When a political figure or personality gets called out for making a snide, race-baiting crack, inevitably the offender is a conservative, and more likely, a Republican; and when Bush and other top GOP leaders drag their feet — or worse, are mute — in denouncing them, Democrats play up their remarks and use that as proof that the GOP is a party of bigots.

The praise by Senate majority leader-designate Trent Lott of Strom Thurmond's earlier days when Thurmond advocated segregation, for example, touched off a spasm of rage in 2001. It took nearly a week for Bush to make a stumbling, kind-of sort-of disavowal of Lott. That was a weak signal to Senate Republicans to dump Lott from his post. It was a strong signal to many blacks that racial animus might still lurk in the hearts of far too many in the GOP.

Three years later, a Rochester, New York, top talk show host and an influential Republican compared the city's black Democratic mayor to a monkey. Shortly after, Massachusetts Senator and Democratic presidential contender John Kerry accused a college Republican group of selling racist T-shirts. Then there was conservative Republican talk guru Rush Limbaugh's cheap grab-at-ratings tirade on ESPN against black Philadelphia Eagles quarterback Donovan McNabb in 2004.

Their outbursts did not represent established thinking among GOP leaders. Their jibes caught GOP leaders flat-footed. They were silent or moved with glacial slowness to denounce the remarks. The sentiment that underlay the casual, and sometimes blatant, racial barbs inevitably percolated down to the troops. Shannon Reeves, a Black California Republican official, complained that as a Bush delegate at the 2000 Republican convention in Philadelphia, even though he wore his delegate's badge and a Republican National Committee lapel pin, he was repeatedly stopped by white delegates and ordered to fetch them a taxi or carry their luggage.

Reeves's account was anecdotal and maybe exaggerated; there are many Republicans who don't utter racist epithets, use racial code-speak, or publicly denigrate minorities, and there is no record that Bush has spoken in a racist vein. But too many Republicans have kept silent about it. That gave civil rights leaders yet another opening to bash Republicans for making — and condoning by their silence — foot-in-the-mouth racist comments and racially loaded attacks.

NAACP Chair Julian Bond took every Republican slight and racially loaded remark personally. He was determined to match every Republican verbal racial insult with his own and slammed Republicans in his addresses to NAACP conventions in 2003 and 2004. His payback outbursts got equally wide media play, and that made many blacks including religious blacks think twice about openly supporting the GOP. Colin Powell openly worried that the racism tag on the party could do irreparable damage to the GOP's effort to sell itself as a party of compassion. He even took a big swipe at his former bosses Reagan and Bush Sr. for what he termed Reagan's at-times "insensitivity" on racial matters and Bush Sr.'s "cheap shot" (his words) in a campaign ad during the 1988 presidential race. In the ad, Bush used a mug shot of black, escaped, and condemned murderer Willie Horton in order to stoke white fears of black crime and hammer his Democratic opponent, Michael Dukakis, as a marshmallow on crime.

In a brutally candid moment, Thomas warned Republicans that they were their own worst enemies among blacks: "Even as someone who's labeled a conservative, I'm a Republican, I'm black, I can say the conservatives don't exactly break their necks to tell blacks that they're welcome." He didn't stop there. He blamed Republicans for "doing things to leave the impression among blacks that they are antagonistic to their interests." Thomas knew his party's recent history well — Goldwater's, Nixon's, and Reagan's real and perceived hostility to civil rights had firmly implanted the notion that when you scratched the surface of a Republican, you would find an unreconstructed bigot underneath.

❖   ❖   ❖   ❖   ❖

Despite Thomas's protests and occasional warnings to Republicans about racial insensitivity, he is relentlessly smeared with the taint of a black man who's propped up by borderline racists. The extreme conservative groups that routinely praise and coddle him read like a who's who of the ultra-conservative right. They have waged war against affirmative action, welfare, and government entitlement programs. Thomas, for instance, is especially close to Paul Weyrich, the head of the Free Congress Foundation, a leading ultra-conservative group. He has made frequent visits to their offices and appeared on the group's National Empowerment Television satellite network. Many blacks perceive the Foundation and the other pro-Thomas groups as thinly disguised racist groups.

The analogy didn't totally hold water. The major civil rights battles of the 1960s were well past by the time that many of the groups that back Thomas appeared on the scene, and even the most conservative groups do not advocate the total dismantling of basic civil rights gains in education, housing, and employment or federal laws that punish racial violence. That should be the minimum that has to happen before tarring a conservative group with the label "racist."

Thomas, however, is not a black academic or a low-level Republican administration appointee. He is an important and visible legal and public policy maker. He often provides the crucial fifth vote on key court decisions on affirmative action, abortion rights, and criminal justice issues. Even when he's on the losing end of a court decision or speaks out against a disputed civil liberties or civil rights issue, his dissent and outspoken opinion stretch the philosophical and legal parameters of conservative ideology and resonate in public policy debates.

Thomas's critics regard his conservative vote as a mortal threat to civil rights and civil liberties. To them, he is the worst kind of hypocrite: He benefited from affirmative action programs at Holy Cross and Yale. He was openly recruited to posts as Assistant Attorney General in Missouri, in the office of education as head of the EEOC, and to the Supreme Court in part because he was black. He then promptly reversed gears and savaged affirmative action programs and claimed that they stigmatized minorities and women as inferior.

That is a glaring contradiction that Thomas is not able to skirt. However, there is no contradiction or hypocrisy in Thomas's evolution from a black student activist to an establishment conservative. The history of black activism is replete with countless examples of blacks who were one-time militant Socialists, Communists, Black Muslims, and Black Panthers in their youth. As they aged, they became militant anti-Communists, super patriots, die-hard conservatives, and mainstays in the GOP.

Thomas swims in the mainstream of black social conservatism. Those ideals, values and beliefs are firmly implanted in black America, and numerous polls have found that a significant number of blacks are social conservatives and agree with Thomas on some social issues, especially tough crime laws, and that more than a few agree with him in opposing affirmative action. The blacks who agree with him are not often heard. They fear being savaged for publicly expressing conservative views. As Judge Keith noted in defending Thomas's right to speak at the NBA affair, they are often bullied into submission. That's at times true, but that's much too simplistic. Thomas and the bevy of black conservative talk show hosts, writers, and political pundits have virtually free license to say whatever they please on radio and TV talk shows.

They carry the odious stigma of being racial apologists for some of the most outrageous bumbles that Republicans make on domestic and foreign policy issues. This erodes their credibility, and opens the gate to the charge that they're mindless yes-men for the GOP. The same could easily be said about black Democrats and their rigid toeing of their party's line on domestic policies. Yet the reality is that the majority of blacks are Democrats, and that makes the Democrats appear to be in the flow of black thinking on political issues while black Republicans seem to be terribly out of step with their thinking.

Thomas solidly established that black conservatives could be every bit the strict constructionists that white conservative judges have proven to be when it comes to interpreting the law. Civil rights leaders discovered that the hard way with Thomas, and they found it out again when Bush nominated black California Supreme Court Justice Janice Rogers Brown to the Federal Appeals Court in 2003. "It's hard to believe that someone can be further to the right than Clarence Thomas," noted People for the American Way head Ralph Neas, "but Janice Brown is."

She terrified Neas and civil rights leaders, and they strapped on the gloves to fight her confirmation. The fight was a lower-intensity Thomas confirmation rerun. Civil rights, civil liberties, and women's groups relentlessly tore into her for her ultra-conservative court opinions and rulings on abortion, tort reform, the death penalty, and affirmative action. They contended that she would wreak havoc on civil rights and civil liberties on the appeals bench.

Her confirmation was hopelessly stalled in the Senate with no sign that Senate Democrats would ever bring it to a floor vote. But then Congressional GOP conservatives hit on the ideal ploy to break the stalemate: They reached back and tore a page from the playbook they used to get Thomas confirmed in 1991. Thomas's chief backer on the Committee during his fight was Utah Senator Orin Hatch. He was there for Brown as well.

He laid a racial guilt trip on Brown's opponents. He claimed that her critics abhorred her not because of her judicial views but because she is a conservative black woman who dared to stand up for her conservative convictions. Brown took the cue and called the attacks on her insulting and implied that she was being singled out because she is a black woman.

The Swift Boat Veterans, the *National Review*, the *Wall Street Journal*, many conservative legal and family advocacy groups, and conservative columnists Sowell and Robert Novak took the same tack. They lambasted Senate Democrats as bigots who tormented a black woman who had overcome segregation and poverty.

The GOP evoked sympathy for Brown by mobilizing black ministers and conservatives, as they did with Thomas. Republican Senate Majority Leader Bill Frist corralled a group of leading black ministers and staged a rally at a park near the Capitol to support Brown. Frist and the ministers proclaimed her a "legal hero" to black America and denounced the threatened filibuster by Senate Democrats. The aim again was to counter the fierce attacks on Brown by the Congressional Black Caucus, the NAACP Legal Defense Fund, and the National

Bar Association. A black rally organizer branded the criticism of Brown by these groups as "partisan rhetoric."

When the chips were down with Thomas, conservatives used race to trump politics. The black-brother-under-attack theme helped narrowly put him over the top in the Senate and onto the high court. Now it was the black-*sister*-under-attack theme with Brown.

The playbook was not outdated. But Brown was deemed unfit to serve on the appeals court, not because she was legally incompetent but because of her conservative views. Brown flunked the liberal litmus test of what a good judge should be. Her great sin was that she thought and ruled as Thomas did on crucial cases that impacted civil rights and civil liberties, criminal justice policy — and she was black.

Yet how else would she, or should she, think? Brown was an outspoken conservative. It was just as problematic for civil rights groups and liberal Democrats to give her a litmus test as a condition for confirmation as it was for conservatives to do the same for judges they deemed to be too liberal. Conservative Senate Republicans had stifled confirmation of some of Clinton's judicial appointments. North Carolina Senator Jesse Helms, for instance, kept nearly a half-dozen vacancies on the influential 4th Circuit Court of Appeals open for years to ensure that Clinton appointees filled none. He stonewalled court selections solely because of their perceived liberal views. And now it was Bush's judges' turn — Brown, for instance.

It was all political one-upmanship. But in contentious political times, a black female conservative judge was especially fair game to be called on the carpet. It took two years and a compromise agreement between Senate Republicans and Democrats before Brown was eventually confirmed in 2005.

❖   ❖   ❖   ❖   ❖

Judge Brown did not become the universal whipping person for civil rights groups. Thomas would always retain that honor. However, he was hardly the only high-profile black the GOP banked on to play a major role in reshaping the political debate within black America. He would apparently also continue to build on Reagan's legacy of cultivating and nurturing other prominent blacks who agreed with and would voice GOP positions on social issues. Well-known conservative blacks could expand the GOP's reach among blacks and help dispel the idea that the GOP was inherently hostile to black interests. To further that goal, the GOP had to smash another racial barrier.

The go-to guy this time was J. C. Watts. In a much-publicized off-year election gambit in 1998, Republicans tabbed Watts the chair of the House Republican Conference. This wasn't a surprise. In 1994, after his election from a predominantly white district, the former University of Oklahoma footballer immediately threw down the gauntlet to black Democrats. He proudly and defiantly declared that he would not join the Congressional Black Caucus.

In one of the keynote addresses at the Republican convention in 1996, Watts also threw down the gauntlet to the old-line civil rights leadership. He punched all the favorite conservative hot-button items, championing family values and self-help and hammering welfare and public housing.

He spotted a potentially significant area of black support for the GOP. By the mid-1990s, many historically black colleges were in desperate shape and had sinking enrollments and chronic funding shortages. It was an issue that was tailor-made for the GOP. Republican presidents from Nixon to Bush Jr. had hailed black colleges as important institutions for black uplift. The added bonus was that, in fighting for black colleges, the White House avoided the contentious battles over affirmative action that wracked major universities.

In July 2000 at a black college summit with black college presidents, Watts and GOP congressional leaders pulled out all the stops to court the presidents. An ecstatic Watts noted after the meeting, "People left their egos, their personalities, and their party associations at the door to make this work." They may have left their egos and personalities at the door, but Watts and GOP congressional leaders hoped that the presidents didn't forget that it was Republicans who were supporting their cause. These Republicans had also turned a canny eye toward the upcoming presidential election. Getting the good will of black college presidents, or at least making them less-than-enthusiastic supporters of the Democrats, would be a big political plus.

Watts continued to goad black Democrats and civil rights leaders. In an intemperate outburst, he branded them "race hustling, poverty pimps." It was a dirty low in mudslinging, and the reaction was swift and harsh. A somewhat chagrined Watts and his Republican mentors rushed to do damage control. He claimed that he was not talking about any one leader or a leader's particular point of view. But he was. The leaders he criticized were civil rights leaders, and their stress was on liberal social programs for blacks.

Watts was not entirely skating on thin political ice in his attacks on traditional black leaders. He knew that by then a growing number of blacks publicly called themselves conservative. There were many more blacks — especially younger blacks in business and the professions — who privately agreed

with some, most, or all of Watts's political views. He also knew
that the old-line civil rights leadership was in crisis. They were
relentlessly battered and bruised during the 1980s and 1990s
by conservatives and were slammed by many blacks for turning
their backs on the black poor.

Watts and the black conservatives believed that time and
the abysslike financial pockets of Republican conservatives were
on their side and that more blacks would eventually rally to
their banner so that black conservatives could then step over
the shattered pieces of the old black leadership to become the
new black leaders. That's especially true in politics, and the
Reagan model of finding and grooming black conservatives for
high profile spots remained the standard for the GOP after Watts
left Congress in 2004.

During and after his congressional days, Watts and some
of the black GOP office-seekers had a daunting problem. That
problem was that while many blacks branded traditional black
leaders as the purveyors of "plantation politics" and called them
sycophants of the Democrats, the majority of blacks still voted
for the Democrats —in fact, most black elected officials are
Democrats.

Clinton did much to solidify that allegiance. By the start of
his second term in 1996, they virtually enshrined him as a demi-
god. The more the Republicans reviled him for his sexual dal-
liances and ripped him for his alleged corruption in Whitewater,
the more blacks rushed to the trenches to defend him. Hard-
line Republican groups also terribly miscalculated in their

tunnelvision effort to eviscerate government entitlement programs.

Even while a number of blacks have reservations — if not outright doubts — about affirmative action, welfare, and other government social programs, they are not prepared to dump these programs. The task for the GOP is to convince blacks that Thomas and other black conservatives are not solely mouthpieces for conservative causes and shallow symbols of the party's commitment to racial inclusion. The one way to do that is to give blacks real decision-making power at all party levels. That was the idea in appointing Watts to a high Republican congressional position.

However, given the towering skepticism of many blacks toward anything the GOP does to reach out to black voters, that's going to be a tough sale, too. Many blacks sneered that Watts's appointment was an empty showpiece gesture and that he didn't wield real power. They were right to reject the GOP pitch if blacks represented the *symbol* of power but not the *substance* of it. Yet, that was not a totally fair indictment. Watts and Thomas did have real clout in the party; Thomas's decisive votes on the Supreme Court and Watts's ability to push the GOP to get increased aid for minority business and black colleges were evidence of that.

Thomas, Brown, and the new crop of black GOP leaders are not going away, and that realization has slowly sunken in among some of their harshest critics. In June 2005, civil rights legend Andrew Young stood beside Thomas on the podium at the swearing-in ceremony of Leah Ward Sears, Georgia's first black female Supreme Court Chief Justice. Later, Young voiced concern about the damage that the internecine war between Thomas and civil rights leaders had caused: "The alienation between him and our community has been unfortunate for all of us."

Despite Young's olive branch gesture to Thomas, the widespread rejection of him by many blacks remains a problem for the GOP. Another problem is that a plan is needed to markedly increase the number of blacks within the GOP's tent beyond the expanding but still relatively small stable of high-end black conservatives — such as Watts, Thomas, Brown, and their prized black senatorial and gubernatorial candidates: Pro Football Hall of Fame receiver Lynn Swann and Ohio Secretary of State Ken Blackwell. There was an obvious way to do that. "If they really wanted to show that they were listening to African-Americans," noted David Bositis, director of the Washington, D.C.-based Joint Center for Political and Economic Studies, "they would take some important issue that's distinctly the issue of African-Americans and run with it." GOP strategists did better than that. They found several issues and a constituency among blacks to go with them.

During Thomas's court confirmation battle in 1991, many conservative black evangelicals cheered Thomas for his opposition to abortion, and they shared his social and family values views. They were the obvious ones to go after. The GOP set the stage for their new political détente by reaching back to the past to make an ideological convert out of the man who is still black America's best-known man of God — Dr. Martin Luther King, Jr.

Chapter 4

The GOP's King Dream

The conga drums beat out a steady, almost hypnotic rhythm as hundreds of placard-waving protesters shouted at the top of their lungs at the man who stood with his head solemnly bowed in front of the tomb of Dr. Martin Luther King, Jr. in Atlanta in January 2004. President Bush, however, seemed oblivious to their taunts as he laid a wreath on the tomb. That didn't quiet the boos and catcalls. In fact, his simple act of remembrance and respect only egged the hecklers on to even more frenzy. In all, the president's quiet pause at King's tomb lasted less than 30 seconds, and Bush strode slowly away with Coretta Scott King, King's widow, in tow.

But the buzz continued even after Bush disappeared from sight.

One of the hundreds of demonstrators loudly insisted that if King were alive he'd have joined their protest. Later Bush, as he has done every year since he took office in 2001, issued a tightly worded statement praising King and acknowledging that King's dream of peace and full racial equality still was unfulfilled. This was more oil on the fire. Bush had just escalated the conflict in Iraq, cut spending on education and job training programs, and done everything possible to arm-twist Congress into dumping a handful of ultra-conservative judges on the Federal Appeals Court who were notorious for their rulings against affirmative action and school desegregation. The greatest issue that drew the wrath of the demonstrators was affirmative action.

January 16, the day after King's actual birthday, it was back in the news. That was the deadline Bush had set to decide whether he would support or oppose lawsuits by two white students against the University of Michigan's race-based affirmative action programs. The Supreme Court would hear arguments on it that April. That was damning evidence that Bush had himself done much to ensure that King's dream went unfulfilled.

An enraged former chair of the Congressional Black Caucus, Elijah Cummings, called Bush disingenuous at best and at worst a hypocrite for trying to wrap himself in King's mantle. Cummings criticism and the gravesite heckling notwithstanding, Bush had moved shrewdly to adopt King's mantle. There was good reason. More than three decades after his murder, King was still the man blacks universally recognized as an authentic

American hero. No other black leader, living or dead, came remotely close.

Bush and conservatives had repeatedly invoked King's name to defend their opposition to race-based programs. They argued that if he were alive he would be on their side and oppose racial preferences. The debate over whether King would have been for or against affirmative action had raged since the 1980s. Conservatives grabbed at King's famed line in his "I Have A Dream" speech at the March on Washington in August 1963 in which he called on Americans to judge individuals by the content of their character and not the color of their skin. Supporters of affirmative action claimed that this deliberately distorted the spirit and intent of King's words. They were both right.

During the furious wars over affirmative action in the 1990s and into Bush's first term, King's words were shamelessly used to justify opposition to affirmative action. Yet there is enough paradox and ambivalence in the few stray remarks that King uttered on the issue to give ideological ammunition to both liberal and conservative camps. At the time, *affirmative action* had not seeped into the nation's vocabulary, and quotas and goals were not issues of public debate. In the 1960s when King spoke about economic destitution and its causes and remedies, he was not referring to discrimination in employment hiring or promotions. He referred to his four children. He was worried that they would be denied equal opportunity because of legal segregation. This was not a visionary declaration but a simple expression of parental concern.

In several speeches and articles during that period, King did not demand that the government and corporations create special programs or incentives exclusively for blacks. With the passage of the civil rights bill in 1964, he realized that ending legal segregation wasn't enough. Integrating a motel or lunch counter did not provide jobs, improve housing, or better schools for the black poor. These were stubborn and intractable problems that required massive spending on new social programs by government and business.

King's debatable ambiguity on affirmative action was only one issue that Republicans could manufacture common cause with him on.

Starting with Reagan, Republican presidents slowly and grudgingly realized that they could wring maximum political mileage out of King's legacy. They could recast him in their image on civil rights, and bend and twist his oft-times public religious Puritanism on morals issues to justify GOP positions in the values wars they waged with blacks, Democrats, and liberals. That wouldn't have been possible if some of King's pronouncements did not parallel the GOP's positions on crime, marriage, the family, and personal responsibility.

❖ ❖ ❖ ❖ ❖

The GOP grab at King's legacy fittingly enough began at the White House. On November 3, 1983, Coretta Scott King stood behind President Reagan at a signing ceremony at the White House as he inked the law that made her late husband's birthday a national holiday. Coretta's face was fixed with a stoic smile as the president penned his signature to paper. The smile was there for a good reason.

The instant that King was gunned down in Memphis in 1968, civil rights and black congressional Democrats demanded that Congress make King's birthday a federal holiday. For a decade and a half, the bill languished in Congress, and the attacks on King's radical politics and character from some conservatives grew more intense. The years dragged by and the bill continued to loll as the battle raged over King's fitness to have a national holiday in his honor. Eventually, mass black pressure and the relentless lobbying efforts of liberal Democrats and moderate Republicans paid off.

Reagan finally signed the bill. But he did so only after it was clear that the bill would pass with or without his backing. Even then, at the 11th hour it took fierce prodding from Vice President Bush Sr. before Reagan threw in the towel on the bill. In a last ditch effort to derail the bill, Reagan said that he would "prefer a day similar to Lincoln's birthday, which is not a national holiday."

Reagan bought into Republican North Carolina Senator Jesse Helms's loud and oft-shouted view that King was not just a noisy racial agitator but also had strong Communist leanings. A month earlier at a White House press conference, Reagan was asked whether he thought there was any merit to Helms's Communist charge against King. The Gipper couldn't resist the sly aside, "We'll know in about thirty-five years." Reagan referred to the voluminous FBI surveillance tapes on King that a court had ordered sealed until 2027. The year after Reagan signed the bill, Helms trailed badly in the polls in his re-election bid. He was thought to be a sure-fire loser. However, he won handily, in part because of hard and at times racially tinged campaigning and a big part of that was his filibuster against the King holiday bill.

Reagan's quip and Helms's rabid opposition sent the not-so-subtle message that King really didn't merit a national holiday. It was also the GOP's Southern Strategy at work again with a vengeance. That entailed ignoring or downplaying civil rights and wooing white Southern males. A decade and a half after King's murder in April 1968, King was still a pariah to many white Southerners, who by then were nearly all staunch GOP backers. Legions of state legislators, local officials, and business leaders instantly took the cue from Reagan's signal that King was still not a man to be honored officially. It took more than a decade, sparked by ferocious political and legal battles and intense opposition from industry groups, before all fifty states finally capitulated and passed a King holiday law.

That did not end the debate over whether King really deserved a holiday. Though many corporations and government agencies plaster full-page ads in black newspapers on King's holiday that extol him and tout how much he's done for them, the MLK holiday is still rock bottom among the national holidays that business and government agencies observe. An annual survey by BNA Inc., a Washington-based business news publisher, revealed that about one-quarter of businesses gave their workers a day off with pay. That number pales in comparison to even the next-least-celebrated holiday, Presidents Day.

The subtle dismissal of King by much of the public and businesses decades after Reagan signed the holiday bill was the hang over from the muddied water that Republicans and conservatives deliberately stirred up when they fought tooth and nail against the holiday — again, while on the surface seeming to embrace King.

Reagan's qualms about King and the holiday bill were another chapter in the GOP's agonizing scorn of blacks. But there was another less well-known side to the flap over the King bill that underscored the torment of the GOP's racial scorn balanced against its need to keep the door open if only ever-so-slightly to blacks. Reagan could have easily vetoed the bill even though he knew Congress would likely override him. That would have curried favor with unreconstructed white bigots and King haters and enhanced his reputation as a man who could not be badgered and bullied into signing a bill he didn't believe in — and he didn't think it was fitting to honor a black agitator. Despite his deep doubts, Reagan in the end may have felt that King was worthy of the honor, and his fight for racial justice was something that Reagan in his own way may have believed in.

Peter Robinson, a Reagan speechwriter and the one who drafted Reagan's speech at the bill-signing ceremony, later said that the words and sentiments he inserted in Reagan's speech — "dignity," "equality," "liberty," "democracy," "freedom," and "fulfilling the promise of America" — were things that Reagan could easily identify despite the political gulf between the two men. Reagan ultimately came to grips with King's fight and the merit of his life. Reagan did something else that showed a true sensitivity toward King: Coretta was hurt and stung by Reagan's crack about King being a possible Communist sympathizer and by his fierce opposition to the bill. He quietly called her and apologized.

At a King observance in 1986, the year after the holiday was first officially celebrated, Reagan seemed to speak from the heart when he denounced racial bigotry and discrimination. The denunciation followed a familiar Reagan pattern: The few times in years past when he was challenged on his racial beliefs or called a bigot, Reagan felt compelled to do a quasi-confessional, bare-the-soul public disavowal of any personal racist sentiment. He told a group of black California Republicans in 1966, "I resent the implication there is any bigotry in my nature."

❖ ❖ ❖ ❖ ❖

The battle over the King bill within the GOP and the tug of war that raged within Reagan over it gave another glimpse into the mildly conflicting and even shifting political thinking in the GOP regarding the importance of the black vote in future GOP plans. In spite of the racially insulting Willie Horton campaign ad that Bush Sr. had green-lighted to help put him in the White House in 1988, Bush Sr. understood that the GOP had to shave off the cruder edges of its divisive racial rhetoric. It needed to adopt a softer approach to racial issues to bump up GOP support among black voters and succeed in its efforts to groom a new breed of black leaders to embrace and push conservative politics.

Reagan and Bush Sr. recognized King's value as a civil rights leader and, more calculatingly, his political value to the GOP. In that sense, King served double duty. His was the name they could voice to get an accolade or two from blacks. At the same time, GOP strategists knew that it was the backlash against the civil rights movement (of which King was still the titular emblem) that had transformed the Republican Party in the South from a political nonentity to a political behemoth.

The GOP benefited from the resonant hostility of many white Southerners to the civil rights struggle. But conservative writers discovered the other part of King's public persona that could be useful — very useful — to make the case that if he were still alive, he'd be in tune with conservative Republican thinking on some issues in the cultural wars. They carefully cobbled together bits and pieces from King's speeches and writings on values issues during the 1950s and early 1960s to paint a King who was anti-big government, welfare, black crime, and an advocate of thrift, hard work, and temperance. This was not a completely politically skewed picture of King.

The urban riots in the middle and late 1960s and the growing white backlash made the GOP's political realignment with King possible. The violence and destruction heightened King's sense of urgency that something had to be done to stem the violence. But King remained ambivalent over how to tackle the problems of the urban poor. In an interview in *Playboy* magazine in January 1965, he was asked if he thought it was "fair" for the government to spend billions on special programs for blacks. King didn't hesitate. "I do indeed." He saw it as a moral imperative that the government "pay back" blacks for the centuries of uncompensated toil during slavery. He bolstered his argument by citing the Marshall Plan, Aid to Appalachia, farmer subsidies, and the G.I. Bill of Rights as examples of the government bankrolling programs to aid specific constituencies.

King did not demand that the federal government create special economic programs exclusively for blacks. Instead, he insisted that special government or corporate programs apply not only to blacks but to the disadvantaged of all races. When the interviewer pressed King on specifics, he continued to hedge. He vaguely called for the government and corporations to increase spending for jobs, skills training, education, and public works.

He felt that the bigger problem for blacks *and* whites was the disappearance of thousands of industry jobs to automation. He sensed that jobs were a volatile issue that could inflame blacks and whites. He claimed that black and white workers suffered equally when jobs were lost and tactfully called on labor to fight for jobs for all.

In the 1960s, affirmative action was seen as a tool to prod employers not simply to hire and promote the disadvantaged of all races as King insisted but specifically blacks. If that happened, King almost certainly knew that this would leave many whites out in the economic cold. This planted the seed of future public misunderstanding and created the huge opening for conservatives and liberals to further squabble over King's words and to interpret them to suit their own ends.

The *Playboy* interview was the first and last time King frontally dealt with affirmative action. He didn't fumble the issue. Those were different times, and affirmative action had not yet stoked the passions that it later would. His words were sketchy thoughts on the issue and were not to be taken as a definitive analysis, let alone a clearly-thought-out, timeless ideological position.

❖ ❖ ❖ ❖ ❖

After the defeat of Nixon in 1960 and the rightward lurch of the GOP, King spoke out more against the GOP's open court of Southern racists. However, his personal conservative philosophy on moral and family values did not change. His solutions to many of the big-ticket racial and class problems that plague America were then and remain a conflicting mix of idealism and hard-nosed pragmatism, but it is on his approach to moral and social issues that King veered closest to the conservative emphasis on family values solutions.

It started with his religious and family upbringing. His social outlook, pragmatic views, and moral values were shaped in great part by the black Baptist Church. The other part was the personal moral strictures that his father, Daddy King, pounded into him in his home, and the Southern tradition of self-help, rugged individualism, and moral self-righteousness and the

Western tradition of personal responsibility. As a divinity student and academic, King flirted with Marxist thought, but he also imbibed the Western philosophical ideals of personal freedom, liberty, dignity, and individual worth.

Even when King castigated President Eisenhower in 1957 for his reluctance to push for tougher civil rights laws and to crack down on Southern lawlessness, he also set his moral compass to chart solutions to the long-standing problems of the ghetto poor — solutions that did not rely solely on government entitlement programs or the passage of more civil rights laws. The same year, in a speech to the Montgomery Improvement Association, King lectured blacks on the value of hard work, the importance of setting personal goals, and striving to develop good character.

In countless speeches in the 1950s, he mingled the demand for civil rights, voting rights, and the government clampdown on racial violence with a forceful call for blacks to practice thrift and self-help, have strong families, and battle black crime and violence. In one speech, he minced no words: "Let's be honest with ourselves, our standards have lagged behind at many points. Negroes constitute ten percent of the population of New York City, and yet they commit thirty-five percent of the violence."

King's criticism, even condemnation, of profligate black behavior was not born exclusively out of his puritanical moral strictures. The occasions when he ventured North on his civil rights forays to make speeches and raise funds, he was appalled at the growing self-destructive and dysfunctional family deterioration and by the high murder rates in urban slums. The passage of civil rights laws and the elimination of Klan violence would not solve those ills. The social pathology in Northern ghettoes shocked and repelled him. He understood that the decades of racism and poverty had seared many blacks with psychic scars. Unfortunately, the victims of the pain those blacks suffered were other blacks.

The broken families, illegitimacy, murder violence, and welfare dependency were taking a mounting toll. In a speech in St. Louis in 1957, he chided blacks that welfare was a dead-end trap that discouraged personal initiative, self-reliance, and personal growth.

As the civil rights battles, demonstrations, marches, and protests gained steam in the 1960s and King hopped from city to city leading marches and protests, he did not fundamentally alter his view that crime, violence, and family breakdown were severe pathologies that wreaked havoc on the black poor.

A year before his murder in 1968, King returned to those themes in his most comprehensive book, *Where Do We Go From Here: Chaos or Community?* Ironically, the book and King's views on the daunting problems of the ghetto poor were largely ridiculed by conservatives or ignored by them at the time.

He was still firmly typecast as a dreamy social reformer — or worse, a loose-cannon radical. But the book provided a clear window into his belief that government programs were not the panacea to solve the problems of poor blacks. King branded the black family "fragile, deprived, and often psychopathic." He made the standard liberal call for more government-funded jobs, education, and skills-training programs.

Nevertheless, King realized that government programs meant little if fathers weren't in the home. This was a major social problem that civil rights leaders either ignored or downplayed. King again strongly emphasized values, training, discipline, hard work, and the reduction of family violence as the key to resolving the family crisis. That crisis increasingly caught the policy attention of liberal and conservative academics and government officials.

❖ ❖ ❖ ❖ ❖

In 1965, Harvard Sociologist Daniel Monynihan dared to say what many whites and a growing number of blacks thought and believed: He called the black family a "tangle of pathology" and dumped much of the blame for that crisis not on racism and poverty but on blacks themselves. It was brash, controversial, and went squarely against the grain of liberal orthodoxy that hitherto had held it as an article of public policy faith that the ghetto poor are hapless and helpless victims of white racist institutions. This sparked loud outcry from civil rights leaders.

Moynihan's blast about the black family was much too broad and his assumptions much too sweeping. He failed to recognize the effects of decades of segregation, economic impoverishment, and government welfare policies that had made the presence of a man a liability in some homes. He also gave almost no shrift to the fact that middle-class black families did not suffer the same alleged tangled pathology as many poor black families. That blind spot earned him the tag of at best insensitive and at worst a racist. Civil rights leaders denounced the study as a ploy to give the Johnson administration an excuse to provide fewer government aid and support programs for the black poor.

Johnson never went in that direction, and Moynihan was certainly not a racist. However, the study planted the seed that the problems of the ghetto poor were of their own making and no amount of government help would do anything to change their plight. They would have to change themselves and that meant blacks had to obtain an education, work harder, stop making babies out of wedlock, and stop committing crimes. That line has become an article of faith in American politics by conservatives, many liberals, and a majority of blacks.

Comedian Bill Cosby trod the same ground as Moynihan when he launched his own moral values crusade in 2005 and stressed black self-improvement. He also implored blacks not to blame whites for any of their failures and not to look to government support to better themselves or as the antidote to poor blacks' social and economic malaise. Cosby's finger-point at the black poor was— as was Moynihan's before him — far too simplistic and dangerously close to victim-bashing. Yet both men's open and implied admonition to blacks to clean up their own moral house was identical to some of King's admonitions that conservatives later used in claiming King for their side.

King did not publicly endorse Moynihan's unsparing dissection of the black family. But he did not join in the cascade of criticism that rained down on him from civil rights leaders either. That was King's tacit way of saying that there were truths in his critique that could not be ignored. At one point, King made an oblique inferential nod to those truths. Without mentioning the controversy or Moynihan by name he chided "a good many writers who have tartly denigrated the role of the family."

The staggeringly high black high school drop-out rate, the widening achievement gap between black and white students in schools, and the wholesale refusal of many black parents to get involved in their children's education could not totally be blamed on racist teachers, and administrators. King implored teachers and administrators to rededicate themselves to the ideal of quality education. He lashed out at lax and indifferent parents who refused to get involved in their children's education.

King returned to a problem that he had harped on continually since the 1950s and that troubled him as much as family breakups and educational dereliction. That was black-on-black crime and violence. Blacks were killing each other in disproportionate numbers in poor urban neighborhoods. That devastating cycle of crime, drugs, and violence tore apart black communities.

Though his priority was on more government-funded job and education programs, he continued to stress family values, personal responsibility, and discipline as a solution to the raging murder violence: "Our crime rate is far too high. We are too often loud and boisterous, and spend far too much on drink. Even the most poverty stricken among us can purchase a ten cent bar of soap; even the most uneducated among us can have high morals."

King would never have dreamed of demanding that welfare be dumped completely. However, he personally disliked it and believed that welfare bred dependency and discouraged personal initiative. He proposed that the government provide direct tax subsidies and tax incentives to corporations to hire and train unskilled workers. That idea was the predecessor of federally backed enterprise and empowerment zones. Republican presidents Nixon, Reagan, Ford, and Bush Sr. backed them and urged that they be expanded. It's the classic conservative free-market solution to chronic inner-city unemployment. It put job creation in the hands of corporations and small- and medium-sized businesses and reduced the government's role in it.

King often quipped that it was futile to integrate a lunch counter if blacks couldn't afford to buy a meal. He demanded huge increases in federal funding for job and skills training programs. But he also recognized that the federal government couldn't or shouldn't do it all. He called for "black dollar days" in which blacks purchased goods and services from black businesses and deposited their savings in black-owned banks. In turn, he expected black entrepreneurs to recycle those dollars into education, recreation, and social programs for the black poor.

This was essentially a recycling of the old notion of self-help and business development as the path to black economic success. During the late 19th century, black educator Booker T. Washington emphasized that message in his self-help and business-friendly speeches throughout the South. In the 1968 presidential campaign, Nixon recycled the idea of economic self-help as the salvation of blacks and formally labeled it black capitalism. Since then, black capitalism and minority business have been the cornerstone of the GOP's program for urban economic development that helped anchor the political ties between many black businesspersons and Republican administrations.

At the Urban League's national convention in July 2004, Bush struck the same pro-business chord: "If you're a small business owner who is trying to expand your job base, take a look at this [Republican] agenda." The audience erupted in sustained applause. In numerous speeches, even into the early 1960s, King continued to stress personal responsibility, economic self-help, strong families, and religious values as goals that blacks should strive to attain.

Republicans repeatedly came back to those same issues as the issues that King felt comfortable with. In fact, the same day Bush was jeered at the King tomb, he skillfully turned the page back on King's call for values, especially religious values, when he stood in the pulpit at Union Bethel AME Church in New Orleans. This was the same church where King had once preached. He told the all-black congregation that he had issued an executive order for the Justice Department to ladle out nearly $4 billion in grants to bids from faith-based organizations.

The reaction from the crowd was far different than the negative response he got at King's tomb earlier in the day. The church exploded in shouts and cheers. Though King would have been a fierce opponent of Bush administration policy on Iraq, civil rights, and social programs, he may well have cheered that announcement too. There would have been no contradiction if he had. King could never be considered a political conservative. Yet the snippets of conservative thinking in his musings on the black family, economic uplift, and religious values blended easily with the social conservatism of many blacks. In the decades after his murder, it blended just as easily into the GOP's prescription for black ills.

Ike met with King. Nixon courted King. Reagan signed a bill that established a national holiday to permanently honor him. Bush Sr. evoked his name in speeches. Bush Jr. praises him effusively on every King holiday. They did that because they and other conservatives found much that appealed to them in King's speeches and writings. That is the part of his legacy that Republicans eagerly snatch at. It is a useful selling point the GOP can use to convince more blacks that King would have stood with them on at least some issues.

King was a black minister — indeed, black America's best-known black minister — and this made his colorblind society and moral values messages even more politically resonant. As the 2004 presidential campaign heated up, the line of communication between the GOP and black ministers sizzled. "We are a people of faith, values, and family," observed Tara Wall, Republican National Committee Outreach Communications Director. "We talked with a lot of black ministers and they agreed with us." This was vital as the party hungrily eyed the black evangelicals as a group that could play a huge role in its battle for permanent political supremacy.

Chapter 5

Courting the
Black Evangelicals

Two weeks after Hurricane Katrina sent thousands of poor blacks fleeing for their lives in New Orleans, the man *Time* magazine dubbed "The Next Billy Graham," noted TV evangelist T. D. Jakes, strode side by side with President Bush on a visit to relief shelters in Baton Rouge, Louisiana for Katrina hurricane evacuees. In the days after Katrina, black leaders had furiously denounced Bush for the government's comatose response to the debacle. Now here was Bush with Jakes in tow. Was this a cheap photo-op to shore up Bush's ruffled image with blacks? If so, why would Jakes lend his name and person to it? Bush obviously had to

say and do something to show that he and the federal government would do everything possible to aid recovery.

Jakes fit in neatly with Bush's refurbished media and public
image. He is one of black America's most recognizable religious
leaders, and Bush had spent months courting, wooing, wining,
and dining black evangelicals. They had become a big and
important cog in the GOP plan to loosen the stranglehold of
the Democrats on the black vote. Though Jakes had never publicly declared his political affiliation, he had long and deep ties
to Bush. Top Republicans regularly appeared at his Potter's House
Church in Dallas. The week before his Katrina stroll with Bush,
he had given the keynote address at Bush's National Day of
Prayer in Washington, D.C.

Jakes was mindful of the knock that he was shilling for the
president in walking around with him. A defensive Jakes told
black reporters, "I want to know that in a crisis when my back's
up against the wall that we can get help to New Orleans as
quick as we got help to Kosovo or Afghanistan." It was a good
point, and Jakes presumably made it in part out of his humanitarian concern for aiding the black hurricane-devastated poor
and in part to send a stern message to the Bush administration
that more must be done to help the poor. This was a subtle dis-
tancing from the Bush administration's foible on Katrina.

Jakes was not about to distance himself from Bush. He and
other top black evangelicals had marched in quickstep with
Bush for years in his conservative morals crusade, and that march
had been very profitable for some. Their churches had received
millions in faith-based dollars for their programs. Katrina did
not sever that relationship, and Jakes's presence with Bush, no
matter how noble and conscientious his motives, sent a clear
message that conservative black evangelicals would continue

to be in the president's camp on at least some issues. The GOP banked heavily on their continued loyalty.

This was not new. The odd symbiosis of God, politics, the GOP, and the black church had been quietly connecting for years. In September 1991, a *New York Times* photo showed dozens of black pastors in a solemn procession on the steps of the Supreme Court building before the start of Thomas's confirmation hearings. The pastors were not there to protest Thomas's nomination — they were there to back it, and they offered their prayers for him. Eventually, the ministers formed a cheering chorus line that snaked through the corridors that led to the caucus room in the Senate's Russell office building. The members of the Senate Judiciary Committee were in there at that moment preparing to grill Thomas.

Civil rights leaders and a legion of Thomas opponents charged that the rally and Thomas support were bought and paid for by the Traditional Values Coalition, headed by California minister and conservative family values stalwart Louis Sheldon.

His avowed mission was to challenge liberals, abortion, gay rights, and pornography. Thomas's opponents were right and wrong — the ministers did jump off buses supplied by Sheldon's group. Sheldon was one of Thomas's loudest backers. But the ministers would not have gotten on the buses if they did not agree with TVC that abortion, gay rights, and pornography were causes to battle liberals on. They agreed that Thomas was the right man to wage that battle on the Supreme Court against those issues.

The pro-Thomas rally was a historic moment and a turning
point for the GOP. The rally served notice to the press, the Sen-
ators on the committee, civil rights leaders, and Democrats that
many black ministers, long thought to be the bedrock of civil
rights and social activism in black communities, were also conservative, and they could be organized for conservative causes.
In the decade after the pro-Thomas rally, Sheldon didn't miss
a beat in his drive to turn black ministers into a political force
in the morals wars. Sheldon didn't shirk from making public
that mission: "We're looking for African-American clergy members
who have local authority, and we're getting them to hold a summit on marriage."

Sheldon's activist push with the black ministers then and
years later demonstrated that black ministers cared as much, if
not more, about family and moral issues as they did civil rights,
affirmative education, and welfare. These ministers and their
congregations numbered in the thousands. They could be a
strong political voice for the GOP and the wedge group that
the GOP had long sought to garner more black support for
Republicans — up to and including, a Republican presidential
candidate.

The black evangelicals who shouted for Thomas's confirmation on the Senate office building steps refuted the popular
and long-standing fiction that the black church from slave times
through the 1960s civil rights era was solidly at the forefront of
civil rights and social activism within black communities.

❖ ❖ ❖ ❖ ❖

The great myth that the black church has always been a
driving force for progressive social change gained widespread

credence during the civil rights movement in the 1960s. During that time, King, Ralph Abernathy, Andrew Young, and the circle of ministers who formed the Southern Christian Leadership Conference rose to national prominence. The press shots of them in 1957 — and the press shots of them in marches and demonstrations against segregation and jubilant civil rights rallies at a handful of black churches in the South — further bolstered the image of the black church as a bedrock of activism.

The secular organizations that King and the other ministers set up were generally not tied directly to established churches. Those ministers willing to take a stand and exert leadership were always in the minority. Many ministers refused to aid the civil rights protests but not because they didn't believe in many of the goals the protesters were fighting for or out of fear — their reluctance to get involved was due to a mix of ignorance, accommodation, biblical dogmatism, and conservatism. In 1961, the rupture over ideology — the role of the church and religion — came to a thunderous head at the National Baptist Convention in Kansas City. This was the biggest and most powerful black religious group in America. The black Baptist group had the allegiance of thousands of pastors and millions of black worshippers. King and a small band of dissidents wanted the convention to play a more active role in the then-escalating civil rights struggles.

The conservatives would have none of it. The convention president, the ultra-conservative, domineering Joseph H. Jackson, sensed the threat to his power and authority. He recoiled at King's challenge to his conservative fundamentalist belief that the role of the black church should be confined exclusively to the business of saving souls, instilling moral and family values, and developing self-help programs. They mounted a fierce counterattack on King and the civil rights-activist ministers. They threatened, cajoled, browbeat, and branded King a "hoodlum and crook."

The convention broke up in pandemonium with physical brawls and even gunplay. King's band of progressive ministers was rudely booted out of the organization. They formed their own minister's group to counter Jackson's conservative Baptists. That wasn't the end of it. A vengeful Jackson banned his supporters and fellow ministers from attending civil rights conferences and events and participating in any activities that had even the faintest tinge of civil rights advocacy.

The civil battles raged over the next few years, and the rifts between the conservative church leaders and the activist ministers deepened. The anger and disgust at the sideline-gazing of conservative black church leaders came to another head in 1966. The National Council of Churches, which included some of the nation's leading socially active black church leaders, took the unprecedented step of taking out a full-page ad in the *New York Times*. The church leaders harshly criticized the conservative black ministers for what they called their "distorted" and "complacent" stress on chariot-over-Jordan sermons while turning a blind eye toward civil rights and the burgeoning black empowerment movement. The conservatives didn't budge.

Many black ministers maintained their sphinx-like silence on civil rights and social issues through the 1970s. The churches stayed riveted on spiritual and moral values, and civil rights didn't fit that bill. The National Baptist Convention in particular even more tightly embraced conservative values and preachments.

In 1984, Jackson made it official when he formally endorsed Reagan. Though Jackson made it clear that his endorsement was personal and did not carry the imprimatur of the Baptist Convention — which by then he no longer officially headed — he took a big shot at the Democrats. He claimed that he endorsed Reagan because Reagan's Democratic opponent, Walter Mondale, represented "entrenched Democrats" who were divisive on racial issues. Jackson didn't elaborate on just how and where Mondale and the Democrats were being racially divisive. However, Reagan's assault on affirmative action programs and his conservative policies did not sway or shake his confidence in and commitment to Reagan and the GOP. It may have even solidified it. The swipe at Mondale notwithstanding, he and his group were fundamentalist churchmen and politically conservative, too. Affirmative action was not an issue that conservative black ministers routinely championed from the pulpit or in their church's publications.

Jackson's successor, T. J. Jemison, took the cue from his mentor and, following a phone conversation and a private meeting with Reagan after Jackson's endorsement, he, too, enthusiastically endorsed Reagan's re-election bid. Jemison and Jackson knew the mood of their flock on key moral issues. The year before Jemison endorsed Reagan, a stormy debate raged over a proposed constitutional school prayer amendment. The GOP backed it, and so did many blacks. In fact, black voters were more fervent in their advocacy of the amendment than any other voting group. School prayer was the first great morals wedge issue of the 1980s that the GOP could exploit to get the ear of black voters.

However, at first it didn't. The rancor between civil rights leaders and Reagan was just too pronounced at the time, and administration officials were not prepared to engage in the kind of political give-and-take with black voters necessary to skillfully exploit an emotional issue — and school prayer was very much an emotional issue among blacks. Perennial black GOP gadfly Alan Keyes sensed that GOP leaders had badly missed the boat on the issue: "If you ask someone whether his kid should be allowed to pray in school, all of a sudden he gets emotionally involved."

Jackson and Jemison's endorsement of Reagan notwithstanding, black churchgoers for the present remained loyal Democratic voters. However, Jackson, Jemison, and the conservative Baptist leaders gave a hint that powerful black religious groups did not regard the GOP as enemies. By the 2000 presidential election, there would be a lot more breathing room for political rapprochement between them. There was no better place to seal the deal with some ministers than at the Republican convention itself. That was evident with a cursory look at the first performing acts on the convention's main stage. It pulsed with black gospel groups and singers. The Reverend Herb Lusk II gave the invocation at the convention. Lusk's Philadelphia church later banked $1 million in federal funds for church-sponsored programs to aid the poor.

Later Mehlman reflected on and took pride in Bush's early efforts to gain more black religious support: "It may not have been 1,000 flowers then, but they're blooming all over the place now, and we'll build on what we've done over the past couple years." They hoped for more black endorsements, support, and votes. It was naked political calculation, but that's what GOP and Democratic Party strategists were in business for.

That the socially active ministers have been the minority among the black clergy — a distinct and notable minority but a minority nonetheless — is not due solely to their religious fundamentalism. More often than not, their social inactivity reflects the traditional social conservatism of their congregations. Studies have consistently found that the greater the religious involvement of individuals, the less likely they are to become involved in civil rights and social causes. In surveys of the professions that have drawn the greatest number of social activists, black ministers ranked dead last in the percentage of those involved in activist causes.

A frustrated King openly chastised his fellow black ministers for their refusal to lift a finger to help civil rights struggles: "Any religion that professes to be concerned with the souls of men and is not concerned about the slums that damn them, the economic conditions that strangle them, and the social conditions that cripple them is a dry-as-dust religion." The phrase was pointed, poetic, and vintage King.

King missed a point, though. Religions, regardless of the color of the minister, are by definition conservative, doctrinary, and textured with moral absolutism. Religion protects traditional family values, regulates moral behavior, tempers social passions, and safeguards the established order. In modern times, the GOP has been the pillar of the political status quo. It has seized and held the morals and family values high ground and fought off every effort by Democrats, as feeble as they've been, to gain an inch of it back. Its stress on family and moral values dovetailed with the fundamentalist black church's rigid moral absolutism.

King and the civil rights protest ministers were not exempt from religion's moral absolutism either. They were militants on racial issues — and, in King's case, peace and social justice issues — but they were every bit as much the conservative puritanical traditionalists when it came to defense of traditional family values, sexual moderation, right-to-life advocacy, spiritual renewal, and personal responsibility as Jackson, Jemison, and their conservative religious nemeses were in the 1960s and 1980s.

❖ ❖ ❖ ❖ ❖

The burgeoning alliance between the GOP and black evangelicals began during the Reagan years. The Republican platforms in 1980, 1984, and 1988 called for "the appointment of
judges at all levels of the judiciary who respect traditional family
values and the sanctity of human life."

Conservatives and Thomas championed the anti-abortion
movement and lobbied hard for strict constructionist judges who
would render anti-abortion case rulings. Since many black evangelicals did the same, it was only a matter of time before the
alliance could formally be cinched. Thomas was the immediate
issue and cause in 1991. If it hadn't been him, Republicans and
conservative black ministers would have found each other eventually on some cause of mutual interest. The *USA Today* poll in
1991 in which blacks backed Thomas by a slim majority had
found that blacks were in tune with the GOP in, for instance,
their opposition to abortion. It also found that hostility toward
gays was greater among more religion-oriented blacks.

Though religious blacks touted family values, most still
didn't vote for Republicans. The majority of black evangelicals
still ranked jobs, the economy, and civil rights and affirmative
action as high priorities. Republican Presidential candidate Robert
Dole and President Bush Sr. barely got 10 to 15 percent of the
black vote in 1992 and 1996 in their losing election and reelection bids against Clinton.

Rock-solid black churchgoers remained wary and distrustful
of the Republicans. But that was not an immutable political fact
of life. Some Democrats recognized the potential and the danger
to their party's political fortunes in any change in any softening
of black attitudes toward the Republicans.

Then Congressional Black Caucus chair Cummings, after a
pro forma castigation of Republican policies, hinted that the negative impressions the GOP had made on many blacks could be

reversed: "If the Republican Party truly meant what it said about opening its doors to the masses of African-Americans, then the party might have more acceptance among black voters." He was a lifetime Democrat, and the last thing that he wanted to see was a marginal black voter shift to the Republicans. Still, his observation hit the mark.

While many blacks have been repelled by the bigotry of some Republicans and are hostile to or deeply wary of Republican policies, some liked or even admired Bush for extending a political hand to them after the 2000 election. Bush wasted little time in his first months in the White House in feting black ministers at the White House and visiting black churches. He didn't summon them for spiritual sustenance or for photo-ops. He had gifts to bear. With much fanfare, he announced that he would get the churches to shoulder a bigger share of the load in helping fight poverty, disease, and promote education programs. The faith-based initiative was the administration's financial ace.

Black churches were targeted in part because they were receptive and open to getting federal money. And they numbered in the thousands. A 1998 University of Arizona survey of 1,200 religious congregations found that far more black churches than white churches would grab at government cash if it were available. It wasn't just the prospect of fattening church coffers that motivated some black ministers, although many of their churches were struggling and in desperate need of any outside money to ramp up church programs. It was a rare chance for them to gain the upper hand from their white conservative fundamentalist counterparts in the hunt to curry favor with Bush: "We are coming out strongly supporting Bush," said prominent black Boston minister Eugene Rivers III, "and we're generating a direct challenge to our flat earth white fundamentalist brothers."

Rivers later had second thoughts about the initiative and slammed Bush for not moving fast enough to ladle out the money. The issue was not the initiative, which Rivers supported, but Bush's failure to finagle money from the government's cash registers for black churches as fast as Bush had implied he would.

Rivers's shot at his "white fundamentalist brothers" was the other part of Bush's calculated targeting of black churches for the faith-based initiative. The top white conservative churchmen didn't want the money. They feared that the money would leave them wide open to federal snooping into their affairs and, ultimately, to their horror of horrors, political control — and that was terribly un-Godly.

Christian Coalition head Pat Robertson voiced that fear: "If government provides funding to the thousands of faith-based institutions, then not only the effectiveness of those institutions but possibly their very raison d'etre may be lost." J. C. Watts instantly saw the political bonanza for the GOP in future elections: "I don't think you'll see six out of ten black people voting Republican in 2002 or 2004, but the faith-based initiative could build bridges."

He strongly implied that the faith-based initiative was a political bargaining chip that Bush could use to boost black support. He couldn't directly say it. That would be too blatant and politically partisan, and it would flatly contradict the White House line. Bush repeatedly claimed that the faith-based program was not political and not partisan. The only criteria to get the funding — for a church or any group for that matter — were need, worth, and commitment — and a viable community-based program.

When Bush dumped University of Pennsylvania political science professor John Dilulio as head of the faith-based initiative program in February 2002, he pointedly said, "There are things more important than political parties, and one of those things is to help heal the nation's soul." Bush bristled at the mere suggestion that the faith-based program was a political payoff for conservative church groups. He told the National Faith-Based Conference in 2006, "I repeat to you, and I'm going to say this about five times, our job in government is to set goals and focus on results. If a faith program is able to get you off alcohol, we ought to say, Hallelujah."

The words were noble, compassionate, and selfless — but they were only words. Bush and the Democrats are consummate political animals who always seek a political edge over one another. In this instance, Bush's faith-based initiative gave the GOP that edge. He intended to use it to maximum effect. There were many cases where faith-based money appeared to be a direct payoff to black ministers for backing Bush. In the buildup to Campaign 2004, the White House shelled out more than $1.5 billion in faith-based money. A handful of black megachurch ministers got millions of those dollars. And, just coincidentally, the bishops and ministers heaped praise on Bush, gave invocations at Republican fundraising events, in some cases publicly switched their political affiliation to the Republicans, and invited Mehlman and a parade of GOP leaders and candidates into their pulpits.

Influential Milwaukee Bishop Sedgewick Daniels heaped effusive praise on Maryland Lieutenant Governor Michael Steele when he barnstormed through Wisconsin campaigning for Bush in August 2004. There were shouts of "amen" and "yes" when Steele told the faithful at Daniels's Holy Redeemer Institutional

Church of God In Christ church, "We know what faith-based can do every single day." Daniels's faith was amply rewarded. He endorsed Bush, Republicans slapped his face on campaign flyers, and he netted $1.5 million in faith-based money.

There was little evidence that the black, pro-Democratic Party ministers got much if any of Bush's faith-based largesse. This angered Reverend Timothy McDonald, a prominent Atlanta pastor. He blasted Bush and the ministers who he claimed were on the take. "It's an attempt to identify new leadership in the black community and use the money to prop these people up."

McDonald was only part right. The faith-based initiative was a handy and serviceable tool to bring selected blacks into the GOP fold. However, Bush's aim (naturally enough) was not to prop up a core of handpicked black ministers to do his bidding but to prop up his reelection campaign.

Bush knew that no matter how hard he pitched his faith-based initiative, the majority of black ministers weren't buying it or him, and those who did were still in the minority among black ministers. At the same moment Bush feted GOP-leaning black ministers at the White House in January 2005, the Congress of National Black Churches drew thousands of delegates from four black Baptist denominations to its meeting in Nashville. The group claimed to represent 15 million black Baptists.

It opposed the Iraq war, demanded a boost in the minimum wage, renewal of the 2007 Voting Rights Act, a big increase in health and education spending, and more aid to the Sudan and Haiti. Their stance on these issues was the exact opposite of the Bush administration's position at that time. Few if any of their leaders were likely to be invited to Bush's White House gatherings or likely to be at the top of Bush's list to get faith-based monies.

In the end, the high-stakes White House political game turned out to be *not* to win a mass following among black ministers — that wasn't likely anyway — but to win an incremental upward bump in the number of black ministers who endorsed the Bush campaign — or, at the very least, for them to remain quietly on the campaign sideline. This was simply hard-gut politics. The Republicans had the money and influence to spread around to get endorsements and votes. The Democrats did the same where they could. Their problem was that they had nothing comparable to offer the conservative ministers.

The Bush administration didn't dangle dollars alone in front of its committed and potential black religious supporters: It also had another huge trump card to play — the cultural and morals wars.

Chapter 6

The Black Morals Wars

The young woman gushed to the cheering black crowd of more than 15,000 faithful that "he" is the new prophet appointed by God to speak the mind, heart and gospel of God. The amens and the yes-sirs were plentiful at the Reverend Bernice King's beatific description of Bishop Eddie Long in December 2004. King is a minister in Long's elegant, stadium-sized New Missionary Baptist Church in an Atlanta suburb, and she had just lit an Olympic-sized torch and passed it to Long at the gravesite of her father, Dr. Martin Luther King, Jr. Reverend Bernice King, Long, and the crowd stood at Dr. King's gravesite to denounce poverty and violence and to stand up for community improvement.

That wasn't the only thing that Long and King called for. He also denounced gay marriage as painful. March organizers deliberately chose King's gravesite to imply that he might well have backed them in their protest. Given her father's relentless and uncompromising battle against discrimination during his life, it defied belief that he would back an anti-gay campaign. He had a close personal and working relationship with March On Washington organizer, Bayard Rustin, who was openly homosexual. The King Center promptly issued a public statement disavowing the Long–King march, and a small group of counter-demonstrators waved placards that read, "Don't hijack Dr. King's dream."

It wasn't the first time that a King family member had evoked King's name and legacy in an attempt to torpedo gay rights. In 1998, King's niece, Alveda King, barnstormed the country speaking at rallies against gay rights legislation. And just in case anyone missed the King family connection, her group was named "King for America." Gay-rights groups everywhere countered King's repent-and-save-yourself message to gays by quoting a public statement Coretta Scott King issued in 1996 in which she noted that King would be a champion of gay rights if he were alive. Coretta had issued the statement to counter the move by a group of black clergy in Miami that had circulated a flier with the picture of Martin Luther King, Jr. to hundreds of black churches in Miami-Dade County in 1996. The fliers denounced gay rights. The group claimed that gays were expropriating the civil rights cause to push their agenda.

❖ ❖ ❖ ❖ ❖

Times, though, had radically changed, and so had the personal and political views of the post-civil rights generation. King's daughter was careful not to mention gay marriage in her talk. Long also cautiously downplayed the issue. In his brief remarks he ticked off hunger, drug abuse, poverty, and corruption as the evils he would war against. There was no mention of gay marriage. Yet Bernice King was an outspoken evangelical, and in the past she and other black evangelicals had marched, protested, written letters, and originated petitions denouncing gay marriage. And she was unabashed in evoking her father's name in the cause: Two months before the Long march, she told an interviewer in New Zealand, "I know deep down in my sanctified heart that he did not take a bullet for same-sex unions."

Long prominently touted Bush's federal amendment banning gay marriage on his church website and was among the handpicked black ministers who met with Bush at the White House. But neither he nor King publicly stated their political affiliations, and neither gave any indication that they actively worked for the GOP either then or in the future. Long bristled at the notion that he was a Bush flack.

King had lent her name to the fight for a key GOP issue and the thought that King's daughter could be a Republican in the making, or even make common cause with Republicans on such a polarizing social issue, caused a mild tremor among Democrats. The White House knew that a strong and growing number of black evangelicals were highly receptive to the Republican moral-values message. If they played their political cards right they could make a crucial difference — even a marginal increase in their support. During the 2004 campaign, Republicans spent millions on ads on black radio stations, successfully wooed a handful of high-profile black preachers, and continually touted the faith-based-initiative program. Bush got at best only a two to three percent rise nationally in black support over what he got in 2000. That didn't mean the money, time and effort of Republicans was a waste. It turned out to be the best bargain of the campaign for them.

The polls also that showed that the prime concern of many blacks was with bread-and-butter issues and that many believed that Kerry was the guy that could deliver the most for them. Polls also showed that a sizeable number of blacks ranked abortion, gay marriage, and school prayer as priority issues for them. Their concern for these issues didn't come anywhere close to that of white evangelicals. However, it was still higher than the concern from the general voting public over these issues. That was especially true on the issue of gay marriage. The issue didn't annoy black evangelicals — it inflamed them. It was contentious, polarizing — but it was also politically useful for grabbing more black support or at least muddying the political waters.

❖ ❖ ❖ ❖ ❖

The first big warning sign that the issue would inflame, polarize, and even energize blacks within and without the black pulpit came in October 2003. At a tightly packed press conference, five of Michigan's top black prelates publicly called on the state legislature to amend the state constitution to define marriage as a union between a man and a woman. The ballot measure passed in November, and more than fifty percent of blacks backed it. GOP strategists knew they had hit the political jackpot. It could gain a few more black votes for the GOP, soften black support for the Democrats — and without the risk of alienating core white conservative Republicans.

An ecstatic Republican pollster Richard Wirthlin rejoiced, "It is an issue that if handled properly can work very much to the advantage of Republican candidates." The Massachusetts Supreme

Court ruling in November 2003 that legalized gay marriage was cause for even further joy by Republican strategists working hard to cement the burgeoning alliance with black evangelicals. A Pew Research Poll taken immediately after the court decision found that far more blacks than whites disagreed with the court's decision.

As the Republican convention neared that August, there was more confirmation that rising black concern over gay marriage could be a lightening-rod political issue for the GOP. A July 2004 CNN/USA Today poll found that far more blacks than whites condemned gay marriage. Civil rights leaders and gay rights activists puzzled at why gay rights had stirred such intense rage among so many blacks.

They piled argument after argument in favor of support for gay rights in an effort to cool black passions over gay marriage. One argument they thought would resonate with blacks was the social and legal taboo against gay marriage.

A similar taboo prevailed for decades against interracial marriage. Interracial marriage ignited hysteria among many whites. Many states banned interracial marriage, and many black men lost their lives to lynch violence over the mere hint of sexual liaisons between black men and white women. In 1967, the Supreme Court dumped all state laws against interracial marriage and declared that "freedom to marry" was a basic right of all Americans. It did not specify that that particular marital freedom should be solely between a man and a woman.

Whether a state tells a couple they can't marry because of their race or because they are of the same sex, it's still discrim-ination. That argument fell on deaf ears with many blacks. The issue of gay marriage pricks several raw nerves. It defies traditional family values. But at a deeper level, it stirs their exaggerated notion of manhood. From cradle to grave, many black men believe and accept the gender propaganda that real men talk and act tough, shed no tears, and never show their emotions.

When black men break the prescribed male code of conduct and show their feelings, they are harangued as weaklings, and their manhood is instantly questioned. They also believe the racial propaganda that manhood is reserved exclusively for white men. In a vain attempt to recapture their denied masculinity, many black men mirror many Americans' traditional fear and hatred of homosexuality as a dire threat to their manhood.

Many blacks — in an attempt to distance themselves from gays and to avoid confronting their own fears and biases — dismiss homosexuality as a perverse contrivance of white males that reflects the decadence of white America. While many Americans made gays their gender bogeymen, many blacks also made gay men their bogeymen and waged open warfare against them. A legion of rappers, black novelists, and poets railed against the gay lifestyle as unnatural and destructive. Many black ministers — as do many white Christian fundamentalist ministers — wave the Bible and rail against homosexuality as the defiler of faith and family values.

The greatest insult that many young black males still level against other black young black males is to call them a "queer," "faggot," or "pansy." These grotesque gender slurs almost always provoke hurt and anger. In a regular season National Basketball Association game in 2001, Philadelphia Seventy-Sixers star Allen Iverson raged at a fan who allegedly shouted racial obscenities at him in a game, mindlessly shouted anti-gay slurs at him. League officials reprimanded Iverson and fined him $5,000. That came on the heels of the release of his rap single "40 Bars," which was laced with anti-gay slurs. Iverson later apologized for his antics, but there was no organized outcry or protest from blacks over his actions.

That was also the case when former street thug and hip-hop and film star 50 Cent told a *Playboy* magazine interviewer, "I ain't into faggots."

Iverson's and 50 Cent's inane slurs could be easily dismissed as the juvenile outbursts of a pampered, spoiled, and untutored jock and of a showboating rapper playing to the street crowd.

The same, though, couldn't be said about Green Bay Packer Reggie White. The perennial all-pro defensive end was thoughtful, articulate, a crowd favorite, and an ordained minister. But in 1997, White touched off a firestorm of protest from gay groups with a rambling, hour-long talk to the Wisconsin legislature in which he took a huge swipe at gay rights and gay marriage. He was promptly dumped from consideration as a CBS commentator. White was unfazed by the furor. He charged ahead with the same ferocity he had used while bull-rushing opposing quarterbacks for years. He turned up at pro-family rallies in several Midwestern cities pushing the anti-gay gospel.

He returned time and again to the theme that gay rights could not be compared to the black struggle for civil rights. At a rally in Iowa in 1999, White pounded Iowa Governor Tom Vilsack for signing an executive order barring discrimination against gays in state agencies: "Every black person in America should be offended that a group of people would want the same civil rights because of their sexual orientation."

Before his untimely death in 2005, White apologized for his anti-gay remarks, but he gave no indication that he had changed his views one whit about homosexuality. He was a conservative black minister, and homosexuality still violated his biblical concept of the proper roles for men and women. In defying the canons of political correctness, White became the first high-profile black evangelical to say publicly what many black religious leaders said and believed. Few blacks joined in the loud chorus of condemnation of his remarks.

Three years before White's headline-grabbing speech to the Wisconsin legislature, a survey measuring black attitudes toward gays was published in *Jet Magazine*. It found that a sizable number of blacks were suspicious and scornful of gays. A 1996 Pew Poll that measured black attitudes toward gay marriage found that blacks — by a whopping margin — opposed it. A CNN poll eight years later showed that anti-gay attitudes among blacks had not changed much since then.

❖ ❖ ❖ ❖ ❖

Civil rights leaders tried another tack to stem the onslaught of black hostility toward gay rights and, at the same time, blunt its use as a political chip for Bush's re-election drive. They vigorously denounced homophobia and urged support for gay rights. They reminded blacks that many of the ultra-conservatives who opposed civil rights also opposed gay rights. This also gained little traction, especially since some of those who vehemently opposed gay marriage also had stellar reputations as civil rights fighters — that is, as long as the civil rights battles were over racial issues. One of those was Walter Fauntroy.

In 2003, the conservative Virginia-based Alliance for Marriage got the backing of Fauntroy and a number of other prominent black churchmen. Fauntroy's civil rights and Democratic Party credentials were impeccable. He had marched and gone to jail with Dr. King and was a founder of the Congressional Black Caucus. He not only endorsed the group's drive for a constitutional amendment outlawing gay marriage but he was a lead-

ing Alliance board member: "I'm unalterably opposed to anything
that redefines marriage as anything other than an institution for
the socialization of children and the perpetuation of the species."
Fauntroy fumed at any talk that he was a stooge of the
Republicans, that he was a turncoat Democrat and a homo-
phobe, and that he had shamefully betrayed the egalitarian
message of Dr. King: "Only fools are going to be diverted to
voting for a Republican on the question of gay marriage, and
we're not fools." Even fools could see that it mattered little
whether Fauntroy personally abandoned the Democratic Party
or even encouraged other blacks to do so: His name on the
masthead of the group that was a stalking-horse in the conservative family values war was a coup for the GOP. It sent a
chill shiver through the ranks of its most avowed enemy, the
NAACP.

At the group's convention in July 2004, NAACP chairman
Bond breathed a huge, visible, and public sigh of relief when
no one demanded that the NAACP take a position, one way
or the other, on same sex marriages. Though Bond had virtually
made a public career out of pillorying Bush and personally supported gay marriage, an open debate on the issue would distract and polarize the convention. That wasn't the only reason
Bond didn't want to see the issue on the convention agenda.
A delegate vote to support gay rights would almost certainly
lose. Revered Julius Caesar Hope, the head of the NAACP's religious affairs department, warned that a resolution to back gay
marriage "would make some serious problems. I would think
the membership would be overwhelmingly against it, based on
our tradition in the black community."

The NAACP would have had egg on its face and would
have been put into the inexplicable and contradictory position
of trying to explain how an organization whose whole history

was dedicated to fighting for civil rights for one group could oppose civil rights for another. The NAACP had dodged the bullet on the issue.

Gay marriage increasingly became a barometer of America's shifting attitudes toward homosexuality, and gay marriage advocates had an uphill battle to convince blacks that tolerance didn't begin and end with race alone. The Democrats had no real defense against the anti-gay phobia among black Christian groups and blacks who weren't of the faith but still loathed gay marriage.

The polls gave early warning signals that the issue could hurt the Democrats. Kerry got twenty percent less support from black conservative evangelicals than Democratic presidential contender Gore got in 2000. Democratic Presidential candidates Al Sharpton and Carol Moseley Braun, during their short-lived bids for the Democratic presidential nomination in 2004, squarely bucked black opinion when they called the fight for gay marriage a civil rights issue.

In the right place and under the right circumstances, black evangelicals posed a stealth danger to Kerry. As it turned out, the right place for Bush was Ohio, and the right circumstance was the state's gay marriage ban initiative. A determined band of activist and outspoken black evangelical leaders backed the ban, and Bush turned the tide for the GOP.

The sixteen percent of Ohio blacks — or about 90,000 voters — who voted for Bush in 2004 and helped put him over the top was significantly higher than the total overall black vote nationally. It proved crucial to his victory on two counts.

If Kerry had nabbed those votes he would have been in striking distance of winning Ohio outright. Even if he hadn't, the loss of those votes would have considerably shaved Bush's relatively slender vote margin over Kerry. He and top Democrats would have thought much harder about conceding the election to Bush as fast as they did. The closeness of the vote would have justified a demand that the election not be certified until the more than 200,000 provisional and absentee ballots were counted. That would have taken days, but it would have kept alive Democrats' hopes that they could still snatch victory from what appeared to be the jaws of defeat. It didn't happen, and it was yet another tantalizing *what if* of presidential elections.

There was no *what if* about the black evangelicals. The helpful nudge they gave Bush in Ohio was not lost on Bush's political architect, Karl Rove, and conservative pro family groups. They publicly declared that they would pour even more resources, time, and attention into revving up black evangelicals in the 2006 and 2008 national and presidential elections. Rove flatly said that Bush would try to pay off one of his debts to evangelicals by pushing the languishing federal gay marriage ban. Family groups said they'd dump gay marriage ban initiatives on ballots in as many states as they could. In some of those states, such as Michigan, blacks make up a significant percentage of voters, and they backed that state's gay marriage ban in big numbers in 2004. Republicans could use the issue to further inflame black anti-gay bias and turn it into support for GOP candidates.

Even if the federal marriage ban ultimately fell flat on its face in future national campaigns and even if Congress never got around to passing it and even if the states never got a chance to squabble over it, the fight over the federal marriage ban could still turn the 2008 presidential elections into a noisy and distracting referendum on the family. That would give Republican strategists another chance to pose as God's defenders of the family and shove even more black evangelicals into the Republican vote column. With the overwhelming majority of blacks still bitter, frustrated, and enraged at Bush for his Katrina foible, Republicans still might capitalize on the gay marriage debate, if for no other reason than to deflect and distract attention from the Katrina debacle and the federal government's laggard role in making things even worse.

In any case, they wouldn't need large numbers of blacks to make the political switch. That was unlikely in even the most optimistic political assessments. A two- or three-point upward bump in the percentage of the black vote could ease the GOP's share of the black vote into the double-digit column. That could make the key swing states of Pennsylvania, Ohio, and Maryland — and New York with a large black voter population — far harder for the Democrats to bag. The core of media savvy, photogenic, politically astute black GOP candidates for top offices in those states could help rally some of that black support the GOP aimed for.

In the flush of Bush's election victory in 2004, evangelical leaders and conservative pro-family groups boasted that the issues of war and peace, jobs, and the economy would take a back seat to moral values in future elections. That wasn't likely. The issues of the Iraq war, jobs, and the economy — as well as failing public schools, crime, and violence in poor inner-city neighborhoods — would always be on the front burner for black voters, most of whom would keep giving Bush a failing grade on his handling of them.

Yet capitalizing on morals issues was only one strategy to bag the top black evangelicals for the GOP banner. The other was to increase the visibility of Bush and Republican luminaries in black communities and at White House meetings and champion issues that resonated with black evangelists. Jake's church was a favorite wayside stop for Republicans in 2004 and 2005. In May 2005, Texas Republican Senator Kay Bailey Hutchinson was one who bobbed and weaved to the beat of gospel music at Jakes's church in Dallas. A week after, Jakes and some of the top names in the black evangelical world trooped to the White House to meet with Condoleezza Rice.

The pastors had mildly criticized the Bush administration for not doing enough to combat the AIDS pandemic in Africa. They wanted Bush to commit more money and programs to fight the dread disease. The Bush administration wanted their names and luster — and their influence with the thousands of blacks who made up their flocks and the countless more who revered their preachments.

The hour-long meeting was inconclusive, and though overt politics was downplayed, politics hung heavily in the air. The mere presence of the ministers with Rice and top administration officials signaled the White House's determination to solidify their détente with top black evangelicals. The prospect of a greater political detente sent shockwaves through the Democrats. New York Democrat Major Owens, a member of the Congressional Black Caucus, voiced the Democrat's fears: "I am concerned that this may be another enticement offered by the administration to African-American clergy." His concern was not unfounded. Though the ministers might endorse the Bush administration's Africa initiative, it did not mean that they endorsed Bush. However, at some point down the road some might, and that potential haunted civil rights leaders and black Democrats.

The mix and match of King's ideology on family values, the social conservatism of the black church, and divisive issues (such as gay marriage) gave Bush and possibly future Republican presidential contenders an opening to score some points with some black voters. However, it remains to be seen whether one or two emotional issues such as abortion and gay marriage will be enough to get a significant number of blacks to back Republican candidates for top offices in future years. The best that can be said is that during the 2004 presidential election, the GOP-leaning black evangelicals forced the Democrats to scramble to find an effective counter to the powerful emotional appeal that religion and social conservatism held among many blacks. They could not simply rely on Bush's stumbles and bumbles to maintain the ironclad loyalty of black voters.

If that didn't add to the Democrats' worries, there was Bush's other trump card, his appointment to and touting of high-profile blacks in top administration posts, with Rice and Powell being the best known. Their names triggered disgust and revulsion in many blacks, but there were others who saw their appointments as a significant breakthrough for blacks — and the GOP knew it.

Chapter 7

Bashing the Icons

In January 2005, Colin Powell was out as Bush's first African-American Secretary of State and Condoleezza Rice was in. In cautious statements as a private citizen, Powell was mildly critical of his former boss for his handling of the Iraq quagmire. However, Powell's belated epiphany came too late. It did not temper the rage that his tenure with Bush had ignited with some civil rights leaders. The bitter feeling some felt toward Powell had exploded in October 2002. It came in an unscripted, off-the-cuff outburst from Harry Belafonte during an eighteen-minute interview on a talk radio show in San Diego. The famed entertainer and civil rights legend called Powell a "house slave" for pushing President Bush's policies.

In his trademark raspy voice, a clearly piqued Belafonte spent much of the time blasting Bush's foreign and domestic policies. That normally would have gotten only glancing notice if Belafonte had simply attacked Powell for promoting the Bush administration's foreign policies.

He had done that often in the past. He and civil rights leaders and black Democrats had repeatedly called Powell on the carpet for misleading the United Nations and the European allies regarding Iraq's alleged weapons of mass destruction, foot-dragging in condemning Sudan's genocide in Darfur, and for shoving African and Latin American development issues to the back burner during his four-year tenure as secretary of state.

Belafonte instead took the easy way out and verbally mugged him as a "house slave": "You got the privilege of living in the house if you serve the master; Colin Powell's committed to come into the house of the master." When pressed later on the CNN's Larry King Live show, Powell, always the consummate diplomat, called his attack "unfortunate." Powell tersely spelled out the acceptable boundary of political attack: "If Harry had wanted to attack my politics that was fine."

Belafonte was not original when he verbally crossed over the line between political attack and personal slander and tagged Powell with the unsavory reference. Malcolm X routinely used the house-slave slur as a throwaway line in his speeches during his Black Muslim days in the 1960s. The reference was to those civil rights leaders — and that for a time even included Martin Luther King Jr. — who supposedly bellied up with white politicians and sold out black interests. Their prime targets were the black political conservatives. It was open season on them. They name-called and personally slandered them with impunity if they dared utter a favorable word about Republicans. That included

Jackie Robinson, Sammy Davis, Jr., and Ralph Abernathy, whose celebrity and civil rights credentials were impeccable. But they had endorsed Nixon and Reagan during their presidential campaigns.

Robinson, Davis, and Abernathy naively thought that in following their hearts and political instincts and endorsing Republican presidents, they would not pay a heavy price for it. They were dead wrong. The GOP's conservative policies riled civil rights leaders and many blacks. The black icons were crucified in the black press and in speeches by civil rights leaders and given a rough cold shoulder by their friends, many of whom they had worked closely and intimately with during the civil rights battles of the 1960s.

There was a big payoff for Republicans. The party discovered that blacks were not politically monolithic and that some blacks, even those admired as legends, would cross the political line, even at the risk of personal ostracism. It was a lesson that the GOP would put to good use in the coming years when it aggressively courted other prominent blacks under the Republican banner. That didn't make things any easier for the prominent blacks who took up the banner. They become prime targets for abuse. As Powell discovered, nothing had changed.

Belafonte's over-the-top blast at Powell as a "house slave" and his subsequent refusal to apologize for it was much more than a personal slander of Powell. It once more pointed up the infuriating tendency by far too many blacks to verbally harangue those blacks who don't toe the line on their brand of racial orthodoxy. Belafonte and Powell's public spat quickly seeped out into the general public. In a CNN quick-vote poll a day after his rip of Powell, nearly 90 percent agreed that his attack was crude and tasteless and appeared more personal than political. Not only did the stubborn Belafonte refuse to back down, he added Rice to his verbal pulverizing. He branded her a house slave too. He told Larry King that they "perpetuated the master's policy." Rice fought back and snapped that she "didn't need Belafonte to tell (her) how to be black."

Belafonte's outburst was not one man's bitter and undignified personal opinion: The name-calling resonated with other black Bush critics. Michigan Congressman John Conyers applauded Belafonte's words: "I have been trying to find where there is something inaccurate about what he said and I can't find it." Belafonte was wildly cheered at the Africare Dinner two weeks later. He received the group's 2002 Bishop Walker humanitarian award. He boasted to reporters that he had done everything he could to get Rice dropped as the keynote speaker at the Awards dinner. She was. There was not a murmur of dissent. The dinner's sponsors, mostly liberal Democrats and civil rights groups, made no effort to distance themselves from Belafonte.

Not all blacks reveled in the Rice–Powell verbal assault. Project 21, a black conservative organization, called for a boycott of the dinner and announced plans to picket it. The sponsors ignored them and publicly reiterated their support of Belafonte. When a group of Project 21 supporters showed up at the Washington Hilton where the dinner was held, they were unceremoniously booted out.

Many other blacks were ambivalent about Belafonte's harsh words as well. The majority of them questioned Bush's policies and many believed that Powell was unable or unwilling to challenge them. They also had grave doubts about whether blacks should be in his administration. But they did not stoop to name calling. In fact, they admired Powell more than any other black leader.

That was consistent with other polls that showed the general was widely admired and had the lowest negative rating among all black leaders and Democratic politicians — and that included the man that many blacks deified, Bill Clinton. Powell's popularity didn't diminish after he left the Bush administration. In a February 2006 AP survey, blacks ranked Powell third behind Jesse Jackson and Rice as the top black leader.

Unlike Belafonte, most blacks were able to distinguish between having political disagreements with Bush and Powell and character assassination of him for his views and GOP allegiance. His support of Bush administration policies was simply too much for many blacks to stomach. No sane African-American, if Belafonte and Powell's other critics were to be believed, could possibly support anything that Bush said or did or any of the GOP's policies. That defied all logic and reality.

Bush's black critics were plainly angered by his domestic policies. But they also harshly attacked Powell, Rice, and the black conservatives out of frustration over the inability of civil rights organizations to have any influence on those policies. In a sense, Belafonte was correct when he used the house slave pejorative — without the slave part. Powell and Rice were in the house, the GOP house. They had influence and visibility, and that gave them a measure of power. Civil rights leaders were further than ever removed from that seat of power.

Months after Powell left office and the controversy with Belafonte had fizzled out, HUD Secretary Alphonso Jackson still dredged up Belafonte's slur against Bush's black appointees to make the point that the civil rights leaders were jealous because they were on the political outs with Bush: "You know the big difference between me and Harry Belafonte and Julian Bond? I am a secretary, and they're not. They'd love to have that as a title. They don't have it." It was hyperbole, and neither Bond nor Belafonte had the slightest tinge of desire to be associated with the Bush administration, but speaking from the aspect of power and influence, Jackson made a point.

By appointing Powell and Rice to important, high-profile administration positions, Bush continued the tradition that Republican presidents had made popular of appointing blacks to political groundbreaking posts. George Mason University professor Walter E. Williams, an economist and a stalwart among the pioneer wave of 1980s black conservatives, observed, "Previous presidents bought and paid for the black vote by appointing blacks to high positions like secretaries of housing and urban development, labor, health and human services, and education."

These were important positions, and the black appointees exercised some policy-making influence in Democratic administrations. Yet, these appointments did not break any fresh ground. Bush did not *have* to appoint Powell or Rice to any position, let alone to two of his administration's top policy-making positions. He got fewer than one of ten black votes in the 2000 presidential contest. Barry Goldwater in 1964 was the only Republican presidential candidate in the last century who did worse than Bush with black voters. Goldwater made such a lousy showing because he backed states rights, opposed civil rights bills, and openly pandered to white Southerners. Bush didn't do that, and that made his miserably low support among blacks even worse by comparison.

Powell and Rice were valued political assets, and GOP insiders knew that they would bring luster and credibility to the administration. There was absolutely no political obligation on Bush's part to appoint them to two of the highest-ranking cabinet and administration positions. The Powell and Rice appointments were by no means political altruism but pragmatic politics. All presidents seek appointees who not only bring talent and skills to a White House post but who also give their administration political cachet.

Powell and Rice's reach extended far beyond the domestic issues. They had become major players on the world stage. That added to the frustration of civil rights leaders. They believed that Powell had a duty to use his influence within the Bush administration to lobby for black interests, which would have meant challenging his boss. In a less heated moment, Belafonte pleaded for Powell and Rice to "speak out about the ill-advised policies." The problem was that his plea for Powell and Rice to use their influence to change Bush's war and domestic policies came as an afterthought. In personally slandering them, he damaged his case and his credibility to make that call. Even that was over-stating the reason for the attack — Belafonte and the civil rights leaders were simply mad as hell that Powell and Rice were in the Bush administration in the first place.

The presumption was that Powell and Rice were mindless automatons and racial window-dressing for Bush. Belafonte made that plain: "They should show some commitment to principles, show some courage." In other words, speak out against Bush policies they disagree with. Congressional Black Caucus chair Met Watt did not begrudge either their right to sit at Bush's table. His gripe was that they wounded black interests by co-signing hurtful Bush policies: "As proud as I am to have a secretary of state be black, if those policies they are pursuing are not advantageous to us, then we have to say that. It's not personal; it's about politics." Watt and Belafonte presumed that neither Powell nor Rice had voiced disagreement over aspects of Bush policy, and even if they did it hadn't changed anything. That was not completely true, especially with Powell.

He was for the most part an administration loyalist and defended some questionable policies such as Bush's deception about Saddam Hussein's alleged weapons of mass destruction. Powell later suffered deep embarrassment and expressed personal regret when the truth came out. The public record also showed that he had said and done much that was at odds with Bush on some crucial policy issues.

Powell bucked Bush and backed affirmative action, urged a formal nuclear treaty ban, prodded increases in economic assistance and HIV/AIDS prevention aid to Africa, and futilely pushed for the U.S. to participate in the U.N. World Racism Conference in Durban in 2001. He also pressed for a formal nuclear treaty ban. If Powell hadn't battled Bush war hawks (Vice President Dick Cheney, Secretary of Defense Donald Rumsfeld, and Paul Wolfowitcz) and argued for a bipartisan, global engagement approach to diplomacy in the months that immediately preceded the administration's final decision to go to war in Iraq, the bombs and missiles would have flown against Iraq with or without U.N. blessing earlier than they did.

An important gauge of the effectiveness of a secretary of state is how well he or she can sell an administration's policy — not to America's international friends, but to its foes. Powell got a reluctant U.N. Security Council to unanimously pass Resolution 1441, which demanded an immediate, fully verified end to Iraq's weapons-of-mass-destruction programs. Even the Syrians endorsed the resolution. Though Powell in an candid moment while still secretary of state said he may have gotten it wrong about Iraq's phantom weapons of mass destruction (he later back-peddled from his epiphany), he still got the UN to go along with Bush's ill-reputed weapons claim. His weapons stance was morally wrong as well as politically disastrous, but the fact that the UN did go along with Powell on it was a tribute to the high regard in which many nations held him. More importantly, it bought valuable time for Bush to prep international and domestic public opinion on the need for war.

Powell may have had little to do with Bush and Cheney's final decision to make war, although there is much dispute about that, but the decision was not his but the president's to make. It then became Powell's job as secretary of state to *not* publicly challenge that decision but to put the Bush administration's best face on it. Even when he mistakenly distorted Iraq's military capacity at the United Nations, Powell still held out for a bipartisan, global-engagement approach on Iraq. He gave the Bush administration's foreign policy sheen and credibility that it couldn't buy.

If Powell were the pawn Belafonte claimed he was, he would not have attained the lofty respect and admiration of European, Asian, and African diplomats. He would not have been in constant demand to attend the top international summits, confabs, and symposia on development issues. When he was jeered at the World Summit on Sustainable Development in South Africa in 2002, the protesters blamed Bush, not Powell, for stonewalling greater development and environmental help to poor nations. The diplomats instantly scrambled to defend him.

❖ ❖ ❖ ❖ ❖

Still, the moment Powell joined the Bush cabinet, the scuttle-butt was that he would never be more than a foreign policy bit-player in the Bush administration. Powell was repeatedly skewered in the media and in political circles as "invisible," "fringe," "impotent," and "ignored" by Bush. The conventional thinking was that Bush kept him around because he was a sop to diversity, had a spit-and-polish image, and was the political favorite of presidents Reagan, Bush Sr., and Clinton.

Powell was loyal to a fault to the presidents he served. So loyal, in fact, that he took a lot of heat for allegedly downplaying the My Lai massacre, deflecting Congressional attention from the Iran-Contra scandal, cheerleading the legally dubious Panama invasion, opposing aid to the Kurds battling against Saddam Hussein, and, most importantly, shilling for Bush's failed and flawed Iraqi war polices.

There were bits of truth in those knocks at Powell. How-ever, they missed the point about his importance to Bush and the complex competing interests that help shape American foreign policy apart from Bush's, or any other president's, ide-ology and world view. Congress — especially the Senate and House Foreign Relations Committee, the various government bureaucracies, the CIA, the Department of Defense, the IMF, key nongovernmental organizations, the major oil, auto, aerospace, and corporations, and banks — have a great deal of say in foreign policy matters.

Powell supposedly was frozen out of the Bush trust circle because of his dustup with Cheney, Rumsfeld, and Rice over Iraq and the terrorism war. They were certainly the issues that dominated the national and international public policy debate after the September 11 terrorist attacks. But they weren't the only big-ticket issues Powell had to deal with during his state department tenure.

Powell got grudging credit for his diplomatic adeptness in helping head off war between Pakistan and India; for his performance at the Johannesburg global warming conference that turned an expected international humiliation into a coup for the U.S.; for defusing the flap with the Chinese in April 2001 when an American surveillance plane was brought down by the Chinese; and for jumpstarting talks with North Korea over its nuclear weapons arsenal.

Chronic Powell watchers repeatedly predicted that he would be out long before Bush's first term ended. They continued to lay the same bet throughout Bush's term, but he lasted the whole first term. He was a valued asset that Bush needed. Powell left because he wanted out, not because Bush told him to leave.

In announcing his resignation to reporters in the State Department briefing room in November 2004, Powell dispelled the rumor that he was a Bush sacrificial lamb: "It has always been my intention that I would serve one term." Kenneth Adelman, a foreign policy specialist who worked with Powell during the Reagan administration, lamented Powell's disagreements with Bush: "The sad part is that he and the president disagreed on national security and foreign policy." That hardly made him Bush's odd man out and the slavish, impotent yes-man held captive to reactionary Republican policies that Powell's black critics insisted he was.

❖   ❖   ❖   ❖   ❖

Those same critics also misread Powell when it came to defying his party on hot-button policy issues. That particular political independence has always stirred the bowels of ultra-conservative Republicans. On occasion, even Thomas publicly bristled at the suspicion by fellow conservatives that he wasn't conservative enough and that he wasn't enough of a team player. In the case of Powell, GOP ultra-conservatives were never awestruck by his general's stars, commanding personality, and public popularity. This was glaringly evident when Powell had made some noises indicating that he might seek the 1996 Republican presidential nomination.

At the time, the GOP had written off the black vote as a lost cause. Clinton had a lock on it, and it was a waste of time trying to loosen his hold on it. But even so, one out of four blacks said they'd still vote for the general, Republican or no, if he ran for president.

Powell's popularity and high ratings with blacks even gave some Democrats faint hope that Powell might be the shot in the arm the GOP needed to make it more responsive to blacks. Kweisi Mfume, then a Maryland Congressman, echoed that thought: "If ever there was an infusion of racial balance needed, the Republican Party needs it, and Colin Powell in that respect helps the party with its perception problem."

The perception that Powell could strike a better balance on race and ethnicity within the GOP made him even a bigger target for GOP rightists. Pat Buchanan and a mighty coalition of conservative groups sternly warned that they would make "war" on him if he were really serious about grabbing the nomination. If Powell had ignored their threat and bulled ahead in his bid for the party's nomination, they would have pounded him for backing affirmative action and abortion rights. They would have dredged up the charge that he did not take Hussein out when he had the chance as chairman of the Joint Chiefs of Staff during the Gulf War in 1990.

The general got their message and quickly opted not to seek the Republican presidential nomination. The secretary of state post was a much better deal for Powell. It gave him a high political profile without the risk of stirring the rancor of the hard right. That meant less than nothing to Belafonte. He and the other black critics would continue to shout "Tom" and "sellout" at Powell to the very end of his tenure in the Bush administration.

In the end, Powell was only the latest high-profile black victim of the tragic but firmly entrenched pattern in which blacks such as Belafonte substituted inappropriate personal attacks, character slanders, and name-calling for reasoned and well-thought-out political criticism and debate. With Powell's exit from the State Department in January 2005, it was now Rice's turn to bear the brunt of criticism.

The assault on Rice came in a way, in a place, and from a person who someone in Rice's position typically did not expect it to come from. It came during a night on Broadway. Audience members at the Schubert Theatre in New York attending the Monty Python musical, Spamalot, rained down boos on her. The boo birds were furious at Rice for being at the theatre the day after Katrina hit. It was clearly a case to them of Rice's let-them-eat-cake indifference to the death and destruction in New Orleans. Rice didn't help matters when a day earlier she went shopping at Ferragamo's, the luxury leather-goods boutique on Fifth Avenue, and reportedly bought several thousand dollars worth of shoes. An incensed shopper shouted at her, "How dare you shop for shoes while thousands are dying and homeless." The shopper was promptly yanked from the store.

Technically Rice bore no direct or even personal responsibility for the Katrina ravage. She was Bush's Secretary of State, and her bailiwick was foreign policy affairs. But she still scrambled to change the public perception that she was unfeeling and uncaring about the Gulf Coast's flood-devastated poor. She embarked on a whirlwind tour of damaged parts of her native Alabama, visited a community center that provided flood relief, and then stopped off at Pilgrim Rest AME Zion Church in Mobile to cheer worshippers on.

Whether Rice made her pilgrimage to grab some camera time or out of genuine concern for the hurricane-suffering residents, Rice was back on the racial hot seat. In truth, she hadn't inched far off the seat since Bush pecked her on the cheek at a White House press conference in the oval office in December 2004. Bush had just announced that he had nominated her for Secretary of State. This was no surprise.

Rice was Bush's most ardent and passionate defender and had gone to bat time and again to defend him from criticism for his foreign policy errors. She took much abuse as the most celebrated and visible black in a controversial GOP administration. A week earlier a white Madison, Wisconsin radio talk-show jock did a poor man's Belafonte imitation and branded Rice an "Aunt Jemima" for allegedly being a white man's lackey. The dime-store high priest of racial correctness also branded Powell an "Uncle Tom."

The Rice bash was too much for a band of black Republicans in Los Angeles. A day before Rice's confirmation hearing in January 2005, press vans lined the streets outside the offices of Justiceville, an organization of homeless advocates. The news crews were there for a scheduled press conference. Ted Hayes, the group's African-American director and a nationally renowned homeless advocate, called the press conference. Hayes also was a staunch Republican and a member of the California Republican Committee.

Hayes was furious at the public catcalling and verbal potshots that civil rights leaders and some in the press had taken at Rice. The criticism was vicious and personal, and it did go beyond legitimate criticism of Rice's politics. She could be criticized for being too hawkish, too fawning toward Bush, too lacking in social and diplomatic graces, and too inexperienced to broker an Israeli–Palestinian settlement and to resolve the crisis over Iran and North Korea's nuclear threat. These crisis issues had simmered during the final two years of Bush's first term. That was fair political criticism from the political opposition. The name-calling was a cheap shot.

The talk-show shock jock was no different from other shock jocks in the business of making off-the-wall cracks about personalities to stir controversy and snatch ratings. But it was harder to dismiss the silence or outright cheers from blacks at his slur of Rice. Many of them burned up talk shows heaping more personal invectives on Rice. The few faint black voices that did publicly condemn the attacks — such as the Madison, Wisconsin, Urban League chapter — were virtually drowned out.

Hayes wanted to correct that and let the public know that many blacks were disgusted at the name-calling. At the press conference, Hayes and a throng of black Republicans, community activists, and local leaders denounced the personal attacks on Rice. Some of the participants noted that they didn't fully agree with her politics and Bush's polices. The harshness of the attacks against Rice also moved Mfume, now the NAACP president, to speak out. While careful not to say anything that could even remotely be construed as endorsing Rice's politics, he rebuked the critics: "(Those) who use stereotypes and racial caricatures are just as bad as those who hide under sheets and burn crosses." The criticism was much needed. He could also have rebuked himself: Five months earlier, in July 2004, in a keynote address to several thousand delegates at the NAACP's 95th annual convention in Philadelphia, he lambasted black Republicans as "puppets" and "ventriloquist's dummies."

He lifted that line from NAACP chairman Julian Bond. Two conventions earlier, Bond used almost the same words to trash black conservatives. He called them ventriloquist's dummies and claimed that they spoke in the "puppet master's voice." Bond also recognized that while name-calling Bush was one thing, there was still the need for a healthy debate on the future of blacks in the Republican Party: "Though we sharply criticize Bush and the Republicans, that's not to say that the Democrats also aren't above criticism either." Still, Bond and Mfume's slurs at the NAACP conventions brought loud cheers and hoots from the predominantly black crowd.

Mfume's milquetoast chide of the Rice bashers was sad testament that Rice was fair game for vicious verbal baiting and name-calling. It was much easier, more fun, and more attention-getting to hack up first Powell and now Rice for allegedly selling out black interests than it was to make a reasoned political case against her administration role. Rice and black Republicans were victims of the double standard of racial correctness. Then-Bush

White House Counsel and subsequent Attorney General Alberto
Gonzales, who is Mexican-American; Housing and Urban Development Secretary Mel Martinez (Cuban-American), and Labor
Secretary Elaine Chao (Chinese) weren't poleaxed by Belafonte
and the other liberal black critics as traitors and lackeys for serving in the Bush administration and for their loyalty to the GOP.

Rice's appointment as Powell's successor to the top foreign-
policy decision-making position stood in stark contrast to the
paternalistic practice of Clinton and other Democratic presidents
to appoint blacks to showy cabinet posts that held little power
or influence. Rice was a Bush administration go-to shot caller.
She was a familiar face and virtually a household name. It was
her job to promote and explain Bush administration policy decisions on North Korean nukes, Iran, the Middle East turmoil, the
war on terrorism, and Iraq.

She was, as Powell was before her, more than a valued
political and policy asset for the Bush administration and the
GOP. She was an ad person's dream. She was articulate and
polished, and the answers she gave to key policy questions on
TV talk shows and in congressional hearings gave a semblance
of credence and believability to Bush's foreign policy miscues.
Rice bought friendship and ideological loyalty to the Bush
political family. She could be depended on to dutifully toe —
and publicly spin — the administration's line, even if it meant
taking public heat for those decisions.

That did happen when former Bush counterterrorism expert
Richard Clarke, in testimony before the 9/11 Commission in
2004, basically dumped full blame for the Bush administration's
September 11 intelligence failings on Rice. She gamely soldiered
on and defended her actions and gave protective answers that
covered the Bush administration's possible response lapses in

the immediate aftermath of the terrorist attacks. Rice proved more than a savvy Bush policy advisor. She was a loyal and reliable political ally. That made her an even bigger target for the black verbal muggers.

❖ ❖ ❖ ❖ ❖

Beyond her role as a Bush loyalist, which earned her both praise and enmity from many quarters, Rice figured prominently in the GOP's racial image remake. At the GOP presidential convention in 2000, much had been made of Bush's pledge to usher in a new racial era for the Republican Party. Rice was a black woman and thus indispensable to the party's promised image remake. This was crucial given the bitter feelings that Bush's 2000 election victory still engendered among many blacks and especially civil rights leaders.

In the aftermath of that win, Powell and Rice became convenient whipping boys for their bitterness. But from the GOP's point of view, they were major assets. Even as civil rights leaders attacked Powell, Rice, and Bush, many blacks privately and even publicly expressed pride in their appointments and the roles they played in his administration. After Clarke attacked her for allegedly falling asleep at the national security wheel, many blacks privately grumbled that Rice would be the scapegoat for alleged Bush intelligence failings.

They consoled themselves that as leading foreign policy decision-makers, they would not be crass apologists for Bush's opposition to affirmative action or for his controversial picks to the federal judiciary. This was not totally realistic. Powell criticized some aspects of the Bush policy. But Rice was more deferential in what she said about his policies, and whatever disagreements she had, she kept to herself. Whether they spoke out or not was their prerogative. They were foreign policy principals, and they had no obligation to speak out on domestic issues.

Powell and Rice's mortal sin in the eyes of their black critics was not that they dutifully defended Bush's much-maligned foreign and domestic policies. They were Republican loyalists, and they were in his administration, so they were expected to do that. Their sin was that they were in the administration in the first place. That made them inviting targets for the verbal abuse their opponents heaped on them.

Bush's policies were no longer the sole issue. The issue was now Rice and Powell. It was the politics of character assassination with a vengeance. The great fear was that by putting Powell and Rice in two of the highest administration posts blacks had ever occupied, the GOP actually meant what it said about making diversity a reality within the GOP. That obviously was not enough to sway the majority of black voters. They were implacable foes of Bush's. The tantalizing *what if* was What would happen if, when Bush is no longer in the White House, Rice made a serious bid for the GOP presidential nomination in 2008? Rice repeatedly said that she wasn't interested, and even laughed off the possibility. Even if she were being coy to deflect and evade the issue of a presidential run, it would not change the political equation much.

Blacks would still vote Democratic. Yet a Rice presidential candidacy would give the GOP a bragging right with black voters, even those blacks who called her names. In an AP poll in February 2006. Jesse Jackson barely edged out Rice for the top black leader spot.

In any case, the appointments of Rice and Powell did break new ground for blacks. For the first time, two black Americans had become architects of international diplomacy and statecraft and had even done their part in making and opposing war policy as administration insiders. Housing and Urban Development Secretary Alphonso Jackson — a close friend of Bush, Powell, and Rice — thought that should count for something: "Black Americans should be pleased that this president has had two black Americans give him the best advice that you can get in terms of handling the war." It did with some, and with others, it was a cause for contempt. In either case, the GOP, Rice, and Powell got the credit and the blame for that.

Their appointments and the controversy they generated was all about partisan politics, which was something politicians could manipulate and control. However, Mother Nature couldn't be manipulated or controlled, and Hurricane Katrina was Mother Nature with a vengeance.

Katrina did more than wallop the Gulf Coast, it also walloped the Bush administration and, at least in the immediate aftermath, forced the GOP to duck, dodge, and figure out what it could do to regain the footing that it had gained using Bush and Mehlman's carefully crafted minority outreach thrust to black voters. That presented another grave challenge for Republicans.

Chapter 8

Katrina Dampens Bush

The floodlights cast a pale, almost eerie light on famed Jackson Square in New Orleans's French Quarter as the man who had much explaining to do about the federal government's laggard response to the Katrina horror prepared to address a national television audience about Katrina. That man was, of course, President Bush. In the days after Katrina struck, FEMA director Michael Brown and his boss, Homeland Security Chief Michael Chertoff, were savagely denounced by civil rights leaders, much of the media, state and local officials in Louisiana, and many in Congress for its foot-dragging response to the disaster. Some Republicans joined in and demanded to know why the government did so little and took so long to aid the disaster-stricken poor on the Gulf. Ultimately, the finger pointed directly at Bush. And a Congressional report in February 2006 and a video released by AP news in March reconfirmed that the administration screwed up mightily.

Bush slightly acknowledged that he and his crisis team made mistakes on the federal relief efforts. But did he do it because the majority of the victims were poor blacks? NAACP President Bruce Gordon, in a gentle, characteristically diplomatic understatement, gave the official civil rights leadership position on Bush, Katrina, and race: "It's clear that the administration has not had (black and poor people) as high on their priority list as they should have."

During her one-stop tour in the hurricane-ravaged Alabama Gulf region, a plainly defensive Condoleezza Rice passionately defended Bush: "Nobody, especially the president, would have left people unattended on the basis of race." However, all the conciliatory words in the world could not replace a vigorous assertion from the president that race was in no way a factor in the government's inept response.

The Jackson Square speech was Bush's chance to silence the critics, and race was clearly on his mind. "All of us saw on television, there is also some deep, persistent poverty in this region as well. And that poverty has roots in a history of racial discrimination which cut off generations from the opportunity of America."

It was forceful, direct, and Bush at least admitted the tormenting reality that race and poverty are organically linked and cannot be swept away. The big question was, What would Bush do about it? Even if he kept his reconstruction promise to pour massive amounts of money into rebuilding New Orleans and the Gulf Coast, would it rinse away some of the bitter taste his initial catatonic response to Katrina left in the mouths of most blacks? Bush knew that he was in trouble and that he had to do more — and do it fast. Aides to Karl Rove worked the phones furiously. They repeatedly called Gordon to assure him that Bush was doing everything humanly possible to get relief to the needy. Time would tell, but for the moment Mother Nature had put a damper on Bush and Republican strategist Rove's relentless drive to elevate their support among black voters. If the presidential election had been held the week after Katrina struck, the mild bump up Bush got in black support during the election would have evaporated. The ultra-conservative black political action group Project 21, which in the past fervently cheered Bush, issued one skimpy press release that mostly attacked the Congressional Black Caucus for racially politicizing the disaster. It made perfunctory mention of the federal response. Bush was not mentioned at all. With the lone exception of Jakes, the few black ministers who ventured any opinion about Bush spoke only of their concern about Bush's mishandling of the disaster and what he'd have do to make amends for it. They were clearly going to wait to see how much of a fight Bush put up to get Congress to pony up the billions for Katrina reconstruction and to combat poverty as he promised in his New Orleans speech.

The potential for a mass defection of his staunchest allies among the black evangelicals worried Bush more than the verbal darts from Jesse Jackson or the NAACP. His conservative and Christian backers were the ones he and GOP leaders banked on to continue to sell Bush's agenda to conservative black churchgoers. The week after Katrina, he put out an urgent

SOS to the most loyal of his black evangelical backers to meet at the White House. Twenty trudged to the meeting and listened politely as a hypercharged Bush repeatedly promised to provide job-training programs, health care, and housing to those left destitute and homeless by the hurricane. The ministers smiled and nodded when Bush cringed at the use of the term "refugee" to describe the displaced citizens of New Orleans.

This was the unfeeling, insensitive, borderline-racist term with which some in the media branded the poor blacks who fled to other cities seeking shelter and relief after Katrina. Bush had heard the term and didn't like it. More importantly, it was his way of scoring political points with the ministers, who plainly didn't like it either.

The administration regarded the meeting a success. The president had put on his most compassionate face, and the ministers were impressed. "There was a feeling that maybe what we have been doing up to now to fight poverty maybe hasn't been effective," said Cleveland pastor C. Jay Matthews, "and we need to move toward long-term solutions." Matthews's willingness to sprinkle his benign assessment of Bush's promises with "we" was proof that Bush had done a phenomenal sales job with the ministers. Bush's stated mission to aid the New Orleans poor had become their mission too. However, it was relatively easy for them to applaud him — they believed in him and in the past supported him. They were as close as Bush would ever come to an audience of true believers among blacks.

Despite Bush's peace overture, in polls taken after Katrina a crushing majority of blacks continued to blame his bungled response to the destruction not on incompetence but on racism. The polls showed that they also blamed Republicans for the suffering. That was more worrisome to GOP strategists than condemnation of a president for incompetence in the face of disaster. The GOP counted heavily on boosting black support in key races in the 2006 fall national elections and hoped to use that success as a springboard to gain even greater black support in the 2008 presidential election.

In the months immediately before Katrina, they had worked especially hard to put the pieces in place. In 2006, their contingent of telegenic blacks bidding for Senate and gubernatorial seats in Pennsylvania, Michigan, New York, and Ohio had the money, name identification, and political clout to win or at least make their races a real horserace. That would draw national attention to their candidacies and boost the GOP. The dangling question in the post-Katrina Bush racial meltdown was whether the candidates could grab a bigger share of the paltry single-digit black vote that Republicans — even black Republicans — had received in state and national election before 2004.

The answer depended on who one talked to. In Pennsylvania, one black lifelong Democrat kept the door open for gubernatorial candidate Swann: "I wouldn't ordinarily vote for a Republican, but who knows? After he gets in office he may do something for his people." Another voter forcefully slammed the door: "The Republicans are backing Lynn Swann because it gives them a chance to say, 'See we're not racist.'" In spite of this skepticism, Republicans could promote a win — or even a credible showing in the races — by Swann, Ken Blackwell, Keith Butler, Michael Steele, and other black Republican candidates to prove that the GOP is a cozy place for blacks.

The Katrina-induced duck-and-dodge away from Bush by many top black evangelicals did not change things. The church leaders remained a key component in Republican plans. By playing hard on the wedge issues of gay marriage and abortion, the GOP needed them to mobilize thousands of their church-going flock to rally around the GOP banner in national elections.

❖ ❖ ❖ ❖ ❖

The Katrina bungle also didn't mean that Bush or the GOP were politically spent with blacks either. Much could happen between Katrina and Election Day in 2006, and Republicans went into maximum damage-control–spin to make sure that good things happened right away. Pennsylvania Senator Rick Santorum kicked off the GOP counter-offensive when he unveiled a GOP poverty reduction program. Bush quickly took the cue.

In his New Orleans speech, he solemnly pledged to make tackling poverty a priority. He squeezed in a big plug for school vouchers, enterprise zones, and greater reliance on his faith-based initiative. These are the standard Republican programs that have received at best light traction. Mehlman stood Bush's bumble on its head and assured anxious Republicans that Katrina was not a setback but a golden opportunity to show that Republicans can wage an effective war against poverty. In a rare White House interview, the president's wife, Laura Bush, got in her licks and publicly demanded that the nation look at poverty in a different way.

The GOP anti-poverty thrust was brazen, opportunistic, and a much-belated effort to seize the political high ground. Nonetheless, it was better by far than anything the top Democrats said or did in the immediate aftermath of Katrina. Massachusetts Senator John Kerry, Democratic National Committee Chair Howard Dean, and John Edwards flailed away at Bush for his Katrina ineptitude, speaking in vague terms about Two

Americas or making a plea for a Marshall-type plan to fight poverty. From the moment the Democrats made the call, the plan was doomed from lack of both money and the political will on their part to push it.

There was absolutely no indication that Democratic House and Senate leaders were willing to fight for the billions it would take to fund a comprehensive program to combat poverty. The Congressional Black Caucus was the sole group among Democrats that showed some zeal for such a fight. During Bush's first term, the Caucus had been nearly totally isolated and marginalized and was unable to get any effective legislation passed.

By *not* putting forth a big, bold anti-poverty plan and *not* showing a willingness to raise their voices loudly and persistently for it — in other words, to be willing and active lobbyists for the poor — the Democrats again let the Republicans off the hook for their stumbles. That's been the sorry pattern with them through two failed presidential elections. The Democrats allowed the Republicans to snatch victory from defeat every time.

Bush would have to do much more than toss out big dollar figures for Katrina reconstruction and talk about fighting a truncated war on poverty. He'd have to deliver the goods. That would determine whether or not the GOP could bob above the Katrina tide with at least some black voters. Six months after Katrina and all the bold talk about piecing things back together in New Orleans, the billions promised still wasn't forthcoming. Bush blamed it on Congress, and Congress blamed it on budget woes. In any case, Katrina reconstruction was still on hold for thousands of displaced Gulf Coast residents.

❖   ❖   ❖   ❖   ❖

Ironically, although Bush and the Republicans got a huge political black eye with even more blacks as a result of Katrina, it was not a total loss. Bush, Rove, and top GOP strategists would never publicly gloat over Katrina's unintended political consequence. Yet, there was a big and potentially lethal one for black voters and the Democratic Party. Nature's catastrophe scattered thousands of poor, black Democratic voters throughout more than 30 states from New Hampshire to California. That could potentially dilute black voter and Democratic strength in Louisiana and the South. Black voters make up one-third of the state's voters and nearly one-half of New Orleans voters. They gave Clinton more than 90 percent of the vote in 1992 and 1996. That propelled him to victory over Bush Sr. and Robert Dole and helped break the GOP lock on state offices in the Southern states he had won.

It also momentarily dented the GOP's Southern strategy. The strategy entailed saying and doing as little as possible about civil rights, actively courting conservative whites, and subtly pandering to the bigotry of Dixiecrat-turned-Republicans. Presidents Nixon, Reagan, and Bush Sr. (in his 1988 win) relied on that strategy to grab the White House. Transforming Louisiana from a safe GOP state with its nine electoral votes into a crucial swing state forced the GOP to pour resources, time, and energy into the state to win it.

While Bush decisively beat Democratic presidential contenders Al Gore and John Kerry in 2000 and 2004, the top-heavy black vote for them enabled Democrats to bag many top state and local offices, but narrowly. A shift of a few thousand votes could tilt those offices back to Republicans in future elections. The loss of thousands of black votes could also crack the thirty years of unbroken black and Democratic dominance of City

Hall in New Orleans. That wouldn't happen in 2006, but the prospect of Democratic defeat in the city was there in future elections. The streets were barely dry in New Orleans's blackest and poorest wards when there was talk that a white Republican would challenge black Congressional Democrat William Jefferson.

If the majority of black voters in Jefferson's district didn't return — and the likelihood was that many wouldn't — that could make the GOP dream of seizing the Democratic Congressional seat more than just talk. That kind of talk worried New Orleans Mayor Ray Nagin. The outspoken, brash Democrat took much heat for his shoot-from-the-lip quip that New Orleans will remain a "chocolate city," meaning that it would remain a predominantly black city. He clearly had an eye on the slight peril that the flight and failure of large numbers of blacks to return would erode the Democrat's loyal political support and give Republicans the opening they hungered for to get greater political control.

The future strength of the black vote in Louisiana ultimately would depend on who and how many came back to the city and state, and when. Many of the mostly white, upscale parts of New Orleans received relatively minor storm damage. The voters in these areas would stay, as would those whose homes were damaged and who had the resources to rebuild them. Many of them are Republican. Thousands of poor blacks don't have the resources to rebuild.

Even if many blacks chose to live permanently in the states they relocated to, that could dilute their vote and further erode their political power. To prevent that, the NAACP and other voter groups called on Congress to pass emergency legislation to extend to displaced Louisiana voters special protections of the Voting Rights Act, which would expire in 2007. The aim was to ensure that they could vote without restrictions in the places to which they relocated. There was no chance that GOP Congressional leaders would do that, and they didn't. They insisted that there were already enough protections to prevent state officials from tampering with voting laws and procedures. The Act currently requires that the Justice Department or federal courts must approve any changes in vote procedures that involve redistricting, district annexation, registration requirements, holding at-large elections, and methods to qualify candidates to safeguard against discrimination.

However, this didn't stop states from making changes in voting procedures that could hurt minority voters, including changing or consolidating polling place locations, tightening voter identification procedures, and adding new and tougher requirements on the timing for filing absentee ballots. State officials claim that the changes were made to prevent fraud or streamline the voting process. There was no evidence that the changes were deliberately made to thin the ranks of minority voters. Still, if minority voters don't have proper identification, have not been informed of polling changes or locations, or don't have transportation to get to them, those voters could be shut out of the voting booth. The identification documents of thousands of blacks cast adrift by Katrina were destroyed or lost in flight.

In the complete absence of polling restrictions or roadblocks, the vote power of the evacuees could still be crippled in the future. Black political strength lay in their numbers and concentration in key states such as Louisiana. Dispersal reduces them to a blip on the political chart in the far-flung states they ended up in. That further waters down their voting strength and potential political clout. "There could no doubt be party advantage associated with it," noted voting-rights expert Richard Engstrom, "that could create more Republican seats in the suburbs."

Rarely in history do political events turn decisively on weather catastrophes. With the passage of time, Katrina may prove to be no exception to that rule. However, in the immediate aftermath of the disaster, it ignited harsh recriminations about the president's performance and, by extension, cast grave doubts on the GOP's ability and willingness to meet the needs of the disaster-stricken poor, the majority of whom were black. They felt bitter and betrayed in their hour of greatest need and desperation, and Democrats readily fanned the flames of racial fury: "We must come to terms with the ugly truth that skin color, age, and economics played a deadly role in who survived and who did not," Democratic National Committee Chairman Howard Dean told the Baptists' Political and Social Justice Commission the week after Katrina.

The GOP didn't need to hear that from Dean to know that Katrina badly hurt them, and whatever momentary gain they might get from the dispersal to other cities of the thousands of New Orleans blacks who traditionally vote Democrat could not make up for the tarnish on the GOP's political image due to Katrina responses. Bush had more to rebuild than New Orleans and the Gulf Region.

Chapter 9

The Twenty Percent Solution

In January 2006, Republican National Committee members hit the ceiling when they got word of a study by Emory University psychologist Drew Westen. Westen did a brain scan of those who self-identified themselves as Democrat and Republican loyalists. He found that Republicans showed more pronounced signs of racial bigotry toward blacks than the Democrats. He did not imply that Bush held any personal racial animosity. In fact, he was quick to add that the president should not be judged by the racial biases of many of his party's supporters. Still, he didn't let him completely off the racial hook. Deliberately or not, Bush appealed to Americans who held anti-black feelings. Republicans screamed foul, and called the study flawed and biased. They pointed out that the study's authors had given money to Democratic candidates. That might have blown away the credibility of the study.

However, another study also showed Republicans were more likely to hold anti-black biases than Democrats. That study was more focused and controlled than Westen's. Volunteers were shown an ad of blacks receiving welfare and another ad on welfare without any racial image. The volunteers shown the ads with blacks were more receptive to Republican political pitches than the volunteers that were shown race-neutral ads. The point was that race did correlate directly with the racial biases of politicians and voters, and the findings dumped at least some Republicans on the racial hot seat. Republican strategists, of course, had spent the last few years struggling to distance themselves from the crude racial appeals that dogged and tainted Republicans for decades.

❖   ❖   ❖   ❖   ❖

In 1989, Republican National Chair Lee Atwater sought to reverse the party's racial course when he boldly announced on CNN's Evans and Novak that the GOP could get 20 percent of the black vote. "It's necessary if we want to truly be a majority party in this country." During the next decade, Atwater's claim was more of a pipe dream than when he made it. The GOP moved even further to the right. Conservatives led by Newt Gingrich captured the House, launched a pro-business, tough-defense, rigid family-values crusade. They warred with Clinton and turned a frigid shoulder to civil rights leaders. By the end of the decade, the party had hopelessly alienated black voters and was well on its way to being an exclusively white party.

If the GOP had any hope of being the majority party Atwater dreamed that it could be, it would have to radically shift
gears and take a step that seemed virtually impossible even as
Atwater voiced his hope for more party diversity. That was to
renounce the race card, ditch the Southern strategy, and pay
more than lip service to reaching out to black voters. In a talk
at the NAACP convention in July 2005, Mehlman was emphatic
that the party's racial blind eye was a major political miscalcu-
lation. "Some Republicans gave up on winning the African-
American vote, looking the other way, or trying to benefit from
racial polarization. We were wrong."

This was not teary, political flagellation, but a hardheaded
political decision, and it was borne on the winds of the changing political and ethnic realities in America. At the close of the
first decade of the 21st century, minorities will make up more
than one-quarter of the nation's population. In the following
two decades, that figure will climb even higher, and Republicans
and Democrats will wage fierce battles to grab even bigger
shares of their votes.

Though Latinos have muscled out blacks as the number
one minority in America, blacks were important bloc voters in
the key states needed by the GOP to maintain its lock on Congress, the White House, and even state houses. Illinois Congressman Jesse Jackson, Jr., sensed the growing threat to the
Democrats: "I've heard Republican strategists argue that if they
could get 15 percent of the black vote, they'd be in power for
a millennium."

The real test came in Bush's close and bitter election in 2004
with his Democratic presidential opponent John Kerry. If Republicans could lop a few points off the Democrat's gargantuan
black vote total, especially in key battleground states, it would

spell the difference between victory and defeat. GOP strategists needed a fresh black political team to get the ball rolling. It had to represent diverse interests and that included black religious leaders, businesspersons, educators, and local GOP political operatives. The team was a more sophisticated replay of Reagan's old strategy of bypassing mainstream civil rights leaders and cultivating a new brand of black leadership. That leadership would be drawn from the ranks of younger, college-educated, articulate, politically independent black professionals and businesspersons. They would be politically astute enough to go head to head with black Democrats and civil rights leaders and to push GOP policies.

In March 2005, the Bush–Cheney Re-election Committee launched the African-American Campaign committee. It got a massive boost of money showered on them by conservative foundations, think tanks, and the GOP national committee, and they were interviewed and quoted on conservative talk radio and TV shows. The team members were mostly younger baby boomers, and they were the true recipients of the post-civil rights era surge in good fortune the black middle class had attained. Many of them were now more willing to lend an ear to the GOP's pro-business, and pro-homeownership pitch.

The shift in political thinking by some in the black middle class surfaced in the 1996 presidential election. In exit polls taken immediately after that year's election, more blacks than whites said that they were better off financially than a year ago and were inclined to self-identify as political independents, if not conservatives.

❖   ❖   ❖   ❖   ❖

There was another reason for their shift. In every election stretching back to Lyndon Johnson's landslide victory in 1964, blacks had given the Democrats more than eighty percent of their vote. Even as an increasing number of Latinos, Asians, and trade unionists defected to the Republicans, blacks stood pat with the Democrats.

Most blacks remained uncompromisingly loyal to the Democrats even when they actively worked against their perceived interests. That was strikingly apparent during the Clinton years. Though blacks hailed him as the honorary black president, Clinton added scores of new death penalty provisions to federal law. America's prisons quickly bulged with mostly black and Latino males, many of whom were convicted of non-violent petty crimes and drug offenses.

He radically downsized welfare, toughened federal anti-crime and drug laws, and pared away affirmative action programs. These were all Reagan, Bush Sr., and Nixon proposals that the Congressional Black Caucus and liberal Democrats vehemently opposed, and they had languished in Congress. However, it was a different story when their titular leader, Clinton, rammed them through Congress. They were mute or offered only token opposition, in part because they were Democrats and they regarded Clinton as one of them. In any case, the black poor were hurt by some of the Clinton initiatives, and the black Democrats that they looked to for leadership again abandoned them.

The ranks of the black poor quickly soared; the numbers jailed for mostly non-violent, non-serious crimes jumped; and funds for skill-and-education programs to permanently break the welfare cycle for the poor evaporated.

Clinton also caved in and dumped his nominees Lani Guinier to head the Justice Department's Civil Rights Division and

Joycelyn Elders as Surgeon General after they got mild flack from conservative Republicans. He did appoint a handful of blacks to administration positions and increased funding for AIDS prevention, minority business, education, and African relief. That was the least that blacks could expect from a Democrat who got most of their vote. But were they anything more than showpiece appointees, as Clinton's black Republican critics claimed?

That charge hung in the air long after Clinton had left office. HUD Secretary Jackson claimed in an interview in March 2006 that he had spoken with two of Clinton's appointees — Secretary of Transportation Rodney Slater and Secretary of Labor Alexis Herman — and that they did not dispute his contention that Jackson had more access to the Bush Oval Office than they had had to Clinton's Oval Office. Was that simply a fiercely partisan appointee's belief, or was it true? Herman or Slater did not publicly dispute it. It can be said, though, that Clinton and Bush's black appointees had the president's ear when he wanted their input on issues, and that held true for many of Bush and Clinton's white cabinet appointees as well.

Civil rights leaders, on the other hand, hammered Bush as the second coming of the unrepentant George Wallace, yet he supported minority business, education reform, and increased AIDS funding and African aid. Bush's Justice Department actually opened more pattern or practice discrimination cases than Clinton did during his last two years in office. Bush's first-administration black appointees Powell, Rice, and Rod Paige held more important administration posts with far greater policy-making power and influence over domestic and foreign policy than Clinton's black appointees ever had.

During the 2000 election, Democratic presidential candidate Al Gore spent most of his campaign avoiding appearances in black communities and was stone silent on issues such as racial profiling, affirmative action, housing and job discrimination, the racial disparities in prison sentencing, the HIV/AIDS epidemic, health care for the poor, failing inner city schools, and drug sentencing reform.

Gore got away with this blatant racial patronizing by playing hard on the terror and panic that the Bush White House win in 2000 had stirred in many blacks. When blacks scurried to vote for Gore out of fear of a Bush, win they gave the Democrats another free ride.

During the 2004 presidential campaign, Democratic presidential contender John Kerry pretty much followed the same cautious script. He once called affirmative action "limited" and "divisive." He did not totally publicly recant his words. If Bush, Thomas, or any other Republican conservative had used that language to describe their view on affirmative action, civil rights leaders and black Democrats would have torn them to shreds. Kerry's campaign website was sketchy about his civil rights aims. In July 2004, he made a tepid and vague call at the NAACP and Urban League conventions for increased support for minority business and job creation and against discrimination and gang violence. Bush had already made the same call.

The tough talk in the Democratic platform and a Kerry–Edwards campaign statement about ramping up military and intelligence spending and hard-target pre-emptive strikes was a transparent effort to trump Bush on his pet national security issue. It was a big tip-off that terrorism and national security — not civil rights or social issues — would be the Democrats' big campaign focus in 2004.

When the crunch came and presidential elections were on the line, Democrats always turned up at black churches, preaching, praying, and belting out "We Shall Overcome." They enlisted an endless parade of black Democrats, athletes, entertainers, and trade unionists to beseech black voters to make a life-and-death sprint to the polls to vote for the party. Gore found out that was not enough to hurdle the apathy and resentment many blacks feel toward the Democrats. Kerry did better, mostly because black Democrats and civil rights leaders pitched the election as a life-or-death holy crusade against Bush.

Now more blacks than ever believed that they hadn't received much in return for their slavish support of Democrats. Bush sensed the disillusionment and actively stoked the flames in a speech at the National Urban League Convention in July 2004. He asked the question, "Does the Democratic Party take African-American voters for granted?"

The answer was a resounding yes, and there were loud cheers. That disillusionment opened up a new world of possibilities for the GOP. The spectacular emergence of the black evangelicals energized by the GOP's anti-abortion, anti-gay rights, and pro-school-prayer pitch as a potent political force was a boon to the GOP.

❖　❖　❖　❖　❖

In spite of the three-decade-long cold shoulder given blacks by the Republicans from the 1960s through the 1990s, many blacks never completely closed the door to the GOP. And though Powell was appalled at the casual racial indifference at times of Reagan and Bush Sr., he gave not a fig of a thought to either making a bid for the Democratic presidential nomination in 1996 or to running as an independent candidate. Polls taken during the presidential campaign showed that a growing percentage of blacks called themselves conservative. If Republican leaders had made any kind of overture to blacks in the 1990s, the number of blacks who would have rushed to them would have swelled their ranks.

Even when Republicans didn't budge from their hardball stand on affirmative action, slash-and-burn of social programs, tax cuts for corporations and the wealthy, and total welfare elimination, many blacks still backed the Republican Party. This was a hint that blacks are not the hardline liberals they have been made out to be. A 1996 poll by the Joint Center for Political and Economic Studies, a liberal black think tank, found that a significant number of blacks favored stiffer sentences for drug use, violent crimes, and three-strike laws and that a near-majority supported the death penalty and school vouchers.

Other polls showed that the majority of blacks backed welfare reform legislation in 1996 as a way to end abject dependency and encourage personal initiative. In the next decade, polls focusing on black voter attitudes showed pretty much the same thing — that blacks were deeply ambivalent and divided on the issues of crime and punishment, education, and family values.

During the 2004 presidential campaign, Bush and Mehlman stood on a historic threshold. They had a real shot at breaking the Democrats' half-century iron grip on the black vote. Democratic Party strategist Donna Brazile tongue-lashed the Democrats for their complacency in the face of the GOP racial onslaught: "Democrats are in the Stone Age when it comes to African-American outreach." Katrina momentarily rearranged the political landscape. The swift, savage, and frenzied fury of most blacks at Bush for his inept handling of relief and failed promises of reconstruction made a temporary shambles of the months of Republican calculation and maneuvering to boost their black support by a few percentage points.

The profound disdain that many blacks have had in the past half century of GOP domestic and racial policies and the Katrina nightmare again guarantees the Democrats a winning hand in the hard-fought game for black voters in the 2008 presidential elections. The question and the challenge for the GOP is whether or not it can do anything to diffuse at least some of the black anger toward the Republicans by then. That will depend on several things.

The GOP would have to continue to groom black candidates for major offices as it did in 2006. It would have to make a serious commitment to put time and resources into the campaigns for those offices. It would have to mount a sustained, ongoing outreach campaign to convince black voters that Bush and Mehlman meant what they said about making the GOP into something more than a cozy good ol' white guys club and also doing more to combat poverty. It would have to renounce once and for all the Southern strategy that Republican presidents Eisenhower, Nixon, Reagan, Bush Sr., and Bush Jr. employed to such devastating effectiveness for decades.

Mehlman barnstormed the country blasting Democrats for taking the black vote for granted and scolding Republicans for their indifference to blacks. In a January 2005 meeting with selected black ministers and business leaders, Bush confidently declared, "If you're looking at which parties give folks the ladder up, the Republican policies are those policies." Bush primed his initiatives on homeownership and small business and pledged to fight to improve health care education and defend Social Security for blacks. Bush banked on these programs to poke more blacks from the Democrats. Katrina didn't change that emphasis.

Not all Republicans, though, bought Bush and the GOP's new race-friendly approach. Thomas Sowell roundly scolded Republicans for bending over too far backward to appease civil rights leaders and black voters: "Why would anyone who wants liberalism go for a Republican imitation when they can get the real things from Democrats?" The only blacks he felt that Republicans should go after are blacks who are anti-affirmative action, pro-life, and pro-smaller government. There are enough of them, Sowell believed, to tilt the balance of power toward the GOP in some states. Ward Connerly took an equally jaundiced view of the GOP's effort to court blacks: "Black people largely continue to view the Republican Party as the 'country club' party rather than the party of the 'common folk,' no matter what station in life they've arrived."

Sowell and Connerly's points were probably only academic anyway. The Republican dependence on the white South to win national elections was the idea that was fixed in the American political mind. More than the other Republican presidents, President Bush has benefited the most from the Southern strategy. In the 2000 and 2004 presidential elections, Bush bagged the electoral votes of all 11 states of the Old Confederacy. In 2000, without the granite-like backing of Bush in these states, Democratic Presidential contender Al Gore would have easily won the White House, and the Florida vote debacle would have been a meaningless sideshow.

In 2004, Bush didn't need the benefit of a Supreme Court ruling on the Florida vote count to hold on to the White House. This time he handily won the South. On the eve of the 2004 election, polls showed that a majority of white Southerners — by whopping margins, especially white males — favored Bush over his Democratic presidential opponent John Kerry. That didn't change even with North Carolina senator John Edwards on the Democratic ticket. The Republican grip was too tight, and civil rights were still a red-flag issue for most white Southerners.

The frozen anti-black attitudes among far too many white voters, the endless legion of black Democrats in state and national offices, and the relentless war civil rights leaders wage against the Republicans (and their imploring of black voters to do the same) have been rigid constants in American politics for the past three decades. This makes make it a tall order — if not impossible — for the GOP to do a total volte face and abandon its core conservative principles.

Still, there was a brief moment when Republicans appeared to be on the cusp of making the long-dreamed-of breakthrough with blacks a reality and give birth to an emerging black GOP majority. Katrina dampened that for the moment. But the imposing array of GOP candidates for Senate and gubernatorial spots in the battleground states in 2006 (and almost certainly in 2008 as well) rekindle hopes that that majority could still spring forth. Yet, even with blacks heading GOP state tickets, without a sustained effort by top Republicans to make diversity a permanent fact of political life within the GOP and win the votes of anything more than a token number of blacks, the emerging black GOP majority will remain a fantasy.

Bush had no thought that it was an inevitability. In a White House meeting with black leaders in February 2005, he sounded almost messianic when he declared, "Our policies offer access to the American Dream to folks who haven't had access." Time and the GOP's actions would determine how much truth there was in those words for black America.

Postscript

In July 2004, President Bush thundered to the throng of delegates at the National Urban League's annual convention in Detroit, "What have the Democrats done for you." It was bold, audacious, and touched a raw nerve. The mostly black and overwhelmingly Democratic crowd erupted in spontaneous applause. The question was not a question but a challenge to black America.

Top Democrats and civil rights leaders sneered at Bush's political dig. At first glance, their sneers seemed justified. There's never been a Republican in the Congressional Black Caucus. Black Republican congressman refused to join. Nearly all black elected state and local officials are Democrats. The top civil rights leaders have always been Democrats.

That seemed to be changing. Bush bumped up his black support nationally in 2004 by several percentage points over 2000. That increase helped put him over the top in the battleground state of Ohio. Bush and the GOP leaders believed that bigger and better things lay ahead. They had good reason to think that. During the past century, the GOP has had a tortured, conflicted, and contradictory but deep and profound relationship with black America. In that century, the GOP pandered to white racists but proclaimed itself the party of Lincoln, liberty, justice, and civil rights. GOP presidents played the race card and used quotas to make black appointments but denounced quotas and championed a colorblind society. GOP presidents used racial code-speak, but railed against racism.

The GOP on the big-ticket public-policy issues opposed Great Society programs, welfare, and government entitlements but backed anti-lynching and civil rights laws, expanded government programs, welfare, and entitlement programs.

The dangling question in 2006 — as it will be in the 2008 presidential election — is whether the GOP can overcome its legacy of racial contention and convince blacks that it offers more to black America than the Democratic Party does. One thing is certain: The historical love–hate relationship between the GOP and blacks presents profound possibilities — and even more profound dilemmas for the GOP.

Essay on Notes

Introduction

The NAACP threw down the gauntlet to Bush and the GOP at its national conventions beginning in 2001. It sensed and feared that Bush might actually do what Republicans paid mild lip service to for a decade and then promptly ignored — namely, actively court the black vote. The GOP now had a core of astute, politically honed, well-financed black GOP operatives and media-savvy conservatives to command attention on the airwaves and in public policy forums.

That posed a serious threat to the Democrats, and Mfume went on the attack: "Mfume calls black conservatives puppets," *Washington Times*, July 13, 2004. Jackson's defense of Bush is in "HUD's Jackson talks tough on Bush administration," *New Pittsburgh Courier*, March 9, 2006. Paige's direct rebuttal to Mfume is in "The NAACP and President Bush, it must be the political season again," thisweekghana.com, August 14, 2005; and "GOP Forms Panel to Draw More Blacks Into Tent," *Los Angeles Times*, March 10, 2005.

Other Republican leaders reminded Bush that the GOP once had attracted blacks: "Bush Doesn't Have to be All Apologies," OpinioNet October 16, 2000 on conservativetruth.org/opinonet/archives.

Pat Buchanan thought the GOP was far too liberal in dealing with civil rights: "the Neocons and Nixon's Southern Strategy," *The American Cause*, December 30, 2002; "Allegations of Black Vote Suppression — Run-Up to Election Exposes Widespread Barriers to Voting," NAACP.org, November 1, 2004; "Soft Sell: Can the GOP convince blacks not to vote?" *The New Republic*, November 11, 2002. Weyrich singed Republican leaders for bad faith toward black GOP candidates in "Black Republican Candidates for the United States Senate," renewamerica.us/columns/weyrich, March 18, 2006. The Black American Political Action Committee, a black conservative advocacy group, still believed that the GOP's racial trump cards outweighed its tainted racial past: "Commentary: The GOP Building Blocks for 2006." blacknews.com, June 27, 2005; Author correspondence with Ward Connerly, March 27, 2006.

Chapter 1 Notes
The Emerging
Black GOP Majority

President Bush repeatedly defended himself from charges that he was insensitive to the plight of Katrina evacuees and the poor and from hip-hop artist Kanye West's blast that he was anti-black at two press conferences in the weeks after the hurricane struck: "Transcript of President Bush's Press Conference," washingtonpost.com, October 4, 2005; "Press Conference of the President," whitehouse.gov/news, December 19, 2005, "Was Kanye West Right?" *Washington Post*, September 13, 2005. Polls showed that Katrina cost him the goodwill he had attained with some blacks: "A Polling Free-Fall Among Blacks," *WP*, October 13, 2005.

The four-year effort by Karl Rove, Bush, and GOP National Committee Chairman Ken Mehlman to boost black support and change the public face of the party are detailed in "Can the GOP Lure Blacks 'Home'," *Business Week*, April 18, 2005; "Blacks Share Spotlight at Republican Convention in Philadelphia," *Jet*, August 21, 2000; "Inside the GOP Mind: How to Win, and Lose Elections" Republican National Convention, *National Review*, August 28, 2000; "Republicans Come Short Courting Black Conservatives," *WP*, January 10, 2005; "GOP Chairman Visits Howard to Lure Blacks," *Black College Wire*, April 4, 2005; "Bush tries to sow doubts about Democrats in Urban League address," *Detroit News*, July 26, 2004. Simmons discusses his meeting with Mehlman: "GOP Chairman's Latest Target for Recruitment: Russell Simmons," blackamericaweb.com, June 19, 2005.

Mehlman talked about his expectations for success in his minority outreach campaign and the GOP's racial polarizing past in "In Case You Missed It: Republicans and the Future; Republicans Apologize for Divisive, Racist Southern Strategy," AP, July 18, 2005; *Washington Times*, January 25, 2005.

The Democrats repeatedly expressed alarm at the GOP's success in courting black independents and the black evangelicals: "Can the polls be right? If they are, black voters are defecting to the Bush camp," *Detroit Daily News*, October 21, 2004; "GOP Courts Blacks and Hispanics on Social Security," *New York Times*, March 20, 2005; "GOP drive to woo blacks via church alarms Brazile," *Washington Times*, March 3, 2005; "GOP woos blacks, but faces troubles," *Detroit News*, May 3, 2005. Hilary Shelton's comment on Simmons is in "GOP Chairman's Latest Target," Ibid.

The GOP faced a huge obstacle in its effort to make the measurable breakthrough it did with black voters in 2004. That obstacle was its own racially exclusionary history in the decade before Bush grabbed the White House. It's amply examined in "Few blacks had roles in recent GOP convention," *Jet*, September 10, 1984; "How blacks participated in the Republican Convention," *Jet*, September 2, 1996; "The GOP's black problem — and the black's GOP problem," *National Review*, December 18, 2000; "Joint Center for Political and Economic Studies Releases News Report on Blacks and the 2000 Convention," *U.S. Newswire*, July 28, 2000; Author interview with Hilary Shelton, April 27, 2006.

By the 1990s, polls showed that more blacks, especially younger blacks, self-identified as political independents and even as conservatives and were receptive to the GOP's pro-business, pro-ownership, law-and-order pitch. Other polls showed the drift of some blacks toward the political center and right. They included the "2004 National Opinion Poll Snaphots: Politics," Joint Center for Political and Economic Studies, September 15 and October 10, 2004; Gallup Poll; *USA Today*, June 23, 2003; "The Death Penalty — American Attitudes," *American Demographics*, November 1, 2001; "Attitudes Toward Crime, Police, and the Law," U.S. Department of Justice, June 1999; "Young Blacks Turn to School Vouchers as Civil Rights

Issue," *New York Times*, October 9, 2000. Republicans and Democrats agree that Latino and Asian voters are and will be a major force in national politics in the years to come and both parties will hotly vie for their votes: "The Coming of the Minority Majority, *Time Magazine*, August 31, 2000; "Minorities increase," U.S. Census Bureau (graph in *Detroit News*, March 27, 2005).

By 2006, the GOP had a stable of bright, relatively young, high-profile candidates it could run in key Senate and gubernatorial races in the battleground states. Republicans banked on them to burnish the GOP's image after the battering Bush's image took after Katrina with black voters: "GOP, Democrats in its sights, grooms black candidates," *NYT*, July 1, 2005; "In Case You Missed It: Swann Typifies Black GOP Seeking High Office inX'06," *Philadelphia Inquirer*, May 18, 2005; and "Swann can't assume he'll sweep the black vote," *Pittsburgh Tribune-Review*, February 7, 2006; Interview with Julian Bond, March 1, 2006.

Black Republican organizations had vastly increased their political reach by 2004. They provided extensive briefing papers, position statements, and news clippings on the slew of black GOP candidates in addition to Parker, Steele, Swann, Butler, Blackwell, and Daniels running for office in the various states in 2006 on its website, theblackgop.com.

Chapter 2 Notes
The Other Reagan Revolution

Reagan even more smartly than Nixon parlayed the "forgotten American" sentiment and a folksy, sanitized image of America's past into a powerful ideological movement. Reagan just as smartly recognized that even as civil rights leaders warred against him (and he against them) that there was a fresh crop of young, upwardly mobile, black business and professional persons who were receptive to his conservative preachments and who could serve as a counter to the civil rights establishment. He moved quietly to corral them.

Two decades later men such as Ken Blackwell were the fruit of his effort. The political odyssey of Ken Blackwell from independent to the GOP is told in "Ronald Reagan's Unlikely Heir," *City Journal*, winter 2006. The statements, speeches, and comments of the principals at the landmark Fairmont Conference are reprinted in *The Fairmont Papers* (San Francisco: Institute for Contemporary Studies, 1981). Thomas's conservative conference epiphany and Reagan's eye on him as a presidential appointee is detailed in "Black Conservatives Meet," *WP*, December 16, 1980; and in Ken Foskett's *Judging Thomas* (New York: William Morrow, 2004), pages 150-156. Sowell lays out his conservative economic philosophy in his books, *Race and Economics* (New York: David McKay, 1975) and *Civil Rights: Rhetoric or Reality* (New York: William Morrow, 1984). Reagan's dictate to get more blacks in his administration is in Foskett's *Judging Thomas* (page 155).

Lewis A. Randolph in "A Historical Analysis and Critique of Contemporary Black Conservatism," *Western Journal of Black Studies*, 19 (Fall 1995) 149-163, and Gayle Tate and Randolph in *Dimensions of Black Conservatism: Made in America* (New York: Palgrave, 2001) give a comprehensive assessment of the deep historical roots of black conservatism. The ten-part series, "Black Conservatives," by the liberal public interest group Political Research Associates is found on publiceye.org, September 1993. It is an unabashed liberal assault on black conservatism and black conservatives. Nonetheless. it provides much valuable information on the personalities, publications, organizations, and funding sources of and for black conservatives.

The mild dust-up between Thomas and Reagan officials over the handling of the New Orleans police affirmative action discrimination case is detailed in Foskett's *Judging Thomas* (168-169). The author assesses the New Orleans case and Thomas's role in it in Earl Ofari Hutchinson's *Betrayed: A History of Presidential Failure to Protect Black Lives* (Boulder Co.: Westview Press, 1995), 178-184.

The *National Urban League State of Black America* (New York: Urban League) reports 1990–2000, and U.S. Census reports tell the tale of black middle-class economic progress. Also see Cecilia A. Conrad (editor), *African-Americans in the U.S. Economy* (Lanham, Md.: Rowman & Littlefield, 2005).

The foundation for the spectacular surge in the numbers and economic expansion of the black middle class were laid during Lyndon Johnson's Great Society program push, Richard Nixon's surprise nudge of affirmative action in his controversial "Philadelphia Plan" to increase the number of black workers and contractors in the building trades, and Jimmy Carter's emphasis on providing black businesses and suppliers with greater access to government contracts and opportunities. See two contrasting views on the impact of the Great Society in "What was really great about the Great Society," washington-monthly.com, October 1999; and Charles Murray, *Losing Ground: American Social Policy, 1950–1980* (New York: Basic Books, 1984). Nixon's controversial affirmative action "Philadelphia Plan" to boost blacks in the trades is discussed in Kenneth O'Reilly's *Nixon's Piano*, 320-321. Carter spelled out his intention to boost minority business in an executive order, "Jimmy Carter: Advisory Committee on Small and Minority Business Ownership, Executive Order 12190" on presidency.ucsb .edu/ws.

Black conservatives parlayed piles of stats to counter civil rights claims that blacks suffered under Reagan: "The Good that Reagan did for Black America," *San Diego Tribune*, June 13, 2004. At the same time the black poor also grew in numbers and desperation during the 1980s; see Gerald David Jaynes (ed.), *A Common Destiny: Blacks and American Society* (Washington, D.C.: National Academy Press, 1989).

Lee H. Walker, president of the New Coalition, a black conservative advocacy group, was also buoyed by the success of the Fairmont Conference. He and six black Republicans paid for a splashy ad in *Jet* magazine urging Reagan's reelection in 1984 in "Blacks, Republicans and Ronald Reagan" on new-coalition.org/Reagan.

Jet founder John H. Johnson typified the pull-yourself-up-by-your-bootstraps, self-made black man Reagan admired. He tells of his admirable struggle to succeed in *Succeeding Against the Odds* (Boston: Warner Books, 1989).

To read about the transformation of the traditional civil rights organization from political activism to economic inclusion for the black businesspersons and professionals — and the opening it left conservatives to pound them as being irrelevant to the black poor — check Joseph G. Conti and Brad Stetson, *Challenging the Civil Rights Establishment* (Westport, Ct.: Praeger, 1993). Walker's Heartland Institute has hosted conferences and symposia and developed position papers devoted to the spread of conservative ideas among blacks. They can be found on his organization's website, Heartland.org.

The debate over the pros and cons of affirmative action during the 1980s and 1990s has been voluminous, exhaustive, and furious. The various sides in that fierce debate have their say in George Curry (ed.), *The Affirmative Action Debate* (New York: Addison-Wesley, 1996), 77-96, and Fred L. Pincus (ed.), *Race and Ethnic Conflict: Contending Views on Prejudice, Discrimination and Ethnoviolence* (Boulder, Co.: Westview Press, 1994), 387-388.

There is thumbnail biographical information on Reagan's top black appointees in Alan Keyes, William Keyes, Samuel Pierce, Clarence Pendleton, and Jay Parker (a pioneer black conservative of the 1950s and early 1960s Thomas regarded as a mentor) as well as their legal woes with Hanes in Walton, "Defending the Indefensible: The African-American Conservative Client, Spokesperson of the Reagan-Bush era," *Black Scholar* 24 (Fall 1994), 46-49; "Black America under the Reagan Administration: A Symposium of Black Conservatives," *Policy Review* (Fall 1985), 27-41; "HUD Secretary Samuel Pierce moves to bolster Blacks in GOP," *Jet*, December 6, 1982; "Former HUD Secretary Samuel Pierce will not be charged," *Jet*, January 30, 1995; "Clarence Pendleton: A Controversial Politician," *The African-American Registry*, www.aaregistry.com; "Clarence Pendleton — The Conscience of a Black Conservative: Interview with Jay Parker," *Insight on the News*, February 19, 2001; and "I just called to say I love you: Blacks and the GOP," *National Review*, November 7, 1986; and "Black Conservatives Grow More Visible," *Baltimore Sun*, July 11, 1991.

The view of civil rights leaders that the Reagan years were terrible times for blacks is found in Steven A. Shull's *A Kinder, Gentler Racism? The Reagan-Bush Civil Rights Legacy* (New York: M.E. Sharpe, 1993). The diametrically opposite view that the Reagan years were times of plenty for blacks can be found in "Black America Under the Reagan Adminstration: A Symposium of Black Conservatives," *Policy Review* (Fall 1985).

Thomas on occasion expressed his pique at white conservatives in various talks and interviews. His quotes criticizing conservatives are in Foskett *Judging Thomas*, 198; Bill Kauffman "An Interview with Clarence Thomas," reason.com/cthomasint; "Why Black Americans Look to Conservative Politicians," Heritage Foundation lecture, heritagefoundation.org, June 1987; "The Burden of Clarence Thomas," *New Yorker*, September 27, 1993.

Chapter 3 Notes
Judging Clarence Thomas

Clarence Thomas in time became the poster boy for the good and bad of black conservatism. But he was hardly the first to become the conservative symbol among blacks. Black conservatism has deep roots in the black experience. Even black leaders such as Frederick Douglass and W. E. B. DuBois who were radical civil rights activists had their conservative leanings. The GOP simply mined the lode of conservative social and economic thought among blacks. Armstrong Williams's showy gala for the older generation of black Republicans was in part a tribute to them, in part recognition of the black conservative tradition, and in part a reminder to civil rights leaders and Democrats that Republican presidents appointed blacks to important administration posts. In some cases, they were breakthrough appointments in "Reception honors black conservatives," *Washington Times*, January 21, 2005.

The National Bar Association and Mercer Law School speeches (in which Thomas lashed out at the notion he was a Scalia puppet and right wing apologist) are in Foskett *Judging Thomas*, 292, 268; and his controversial votes on death penalty cases — in one such case Scalia did not agree with him — are detailed in "Justice Embraces Image as a Hard-Line Holdout," *WP*, October 12, 2004; and "Supreme Court's race bias rulings opposed by black justice," AP, June 14, 2005. The Thomas–NAACP school controversy and the sparring match with Leon Higginbotham at the NBA conference are recounted in "Judge Thomas Withdraws from Banquet Appearance," *AllPolitics*, January 8, 1997 and "For Clarence Thomas, Another Invitation and Another Flap," *WP*, June 18, 1998. Howard Ball assesses the relationship between Brennan and Marshall in *A Defiant Life: Thurgood Marshall & the Persistence of American Racism* (New York: Crown Books 1998), 210-211.

The furor over Trent Lott's pro-segregation praise of former South Carolina Senator Strom Thurmond and Rush Limbaugh and the racial gaffes of conservatives was the subject of intense reporting and commentary in the *Washington Post, New York Times,* and *Los Angeles Times,* and black newspapers and on liberal and left activist websites such as Alternet.org. Shannon Reeves poured out his heart to GOP officials about racial slights in "Open Letter to the Board of the California Republican Party," freerepublic.com/focus, January 9, 2003. Powell took a mild swipe at Reagan and Bush Sr. for their racial "insensitivity" in *My Journey,* 400; Thomas also got his dig in at white conservatives for racial hostility in the interview in reason.com/cthomasint.

The furious battle over Thomas's Supreme Court confirmation has been told innumerable times. Despite its unapologetic anti-Thomas, pro-Anita Hill bias, Jane Meyer and Jill Abramson's, *Strange Justice: The Selling of Clarence Thomas* (New York: Houghton-Mifflin, 1994; 186-187, 201, 286, 356) is still the best account of the titanic fight as well as a detailed biographical sketch of Thomas's pre-Supreme Court days; and "Clarence Thomas offers a glimpse of his thoughts: he regrets the controversy over his confirmation hearings," *Philadelphia Inquirer,* May 12, 2003. For background on the Free Congress Foundation, see the group's website, freecongress.org.

Weyrich accused GOP leaders of subverting the candidacies of prominent black Republican candidates for Senate and gubernatorial spots in the fall 2006 elections in "Black Republican Candidates for the United States Senate," renewamerica.us/columns.weyrich, March 18, 2006.

There is as yet no definitive biography of Judge Janice Rogers Brown. However, during the confirmation fight over her appeals court nomination, a sketch of her career and her views were detailed and examined by her critics in "Judge Brown: She is on the Right, and Many say, in the Wrong," Issues and Views, *The Crisis*, November/December, 2003; "Congressional Black Caucus Urges U.S. Senate to Reject Brown," CBC News Release, June 6, 2005.

A look at Watts's life — the controversies he was embroiled in, the criticisms of him, and the initiatives he pushed, especially greater funding for Historically Black Colleges — are found in "The GOP's Shining Star" *Washington Monthly*, October 1996; "Black, Proud — and Republican," *Economist* 335 (April 1, 1995); "Republican like Me," *National Review*, April 22, 1996; J. C. Watts, *What Color is a Conservative: My Life and My Politics* (New York: Perennial Press, 2003); and "Unlikely Alliances: HBCU officials Meet with GOP Leaders," *Black Issues in Higher Education*, July 6, 2000.

Young's momentary détente with Thomas is in "Thomas Goes Home for Swearing In," *LAT*, June 29, 2005; Bositis's quote on what Republicans must do to attract more blacks is in "GOP woos blacks, but faces struggle," *Detroit News*, March 27, 2005.

Chapter 4 Notes
The GOP's King Dream

Since the 1980s, the GOP has been relentless in its effort to claim a part of Martin Luther King, Jr.'s legacy. The three great issues in which it sought to wrap itself tightly with his views were affirmative action, moral values, and opposition to gay rights. King's daughter, Bernice, brought the gay rights controversy issue to a head with her march to her father's gravesite with Atlanta Bishop Eddie Long.

There were a number of press accounts of that march and the reaction to it. The most detailed fittingly was in King's hometown paper, *Atlanta Constitution*: "March pushes moral Agenda," December 12, 2004; "Gay-marriage advocates protest King march," AP, December 11, 2004. Reagan and the controversy he kicked up over the King holiday bill and his later public recrimination about it in Lou Cannon's *President Reagan: The Role of a Lifetime* (New York: Simon & Schuster, 1991; 524); and Taylor Branch *At Canaan's Edge*, 480-81; Kiron Skinner *NYT*, January 19, 2004; the BNA annual business surveys on the still-widespread resistance to the King holiday can be found on its website, bna.com/press/2006/mlkday.

King's sketchy views on affirmative action and the problems of the urban poor are in his *Where Do We Go from Here? Chaos or Community* (New York: Harper & Row Publishers, 1967); "Playboy Interview: Martin Luther King," *Playboy*, January 1965; "Next Stop: The North," *Saturday Review,* 48, November 13, 1965. King's 1950s moral preachments on family values, black crime, and religious values are in his *Strength to Love* (New York: Harper & Row, 1963); "Where Dr. King Went Wrong," *City Journal*, Winter 2002; "King's Conservative Mind," nationalreview.com, January 21, 2002.

Moynihan propounds his thesis about the black family crisis and its alleged pathology in *The Negro Family: The Case for National Action* (Washington, D.C.: U.S. Government Printing Office, 1965); and the controversy over it is in "The Black Family: Forty Years of Lies," *City Journal*, Summer 2005.

Four decades later, Bill Cosby echoed Moynihan in his blast at underachieving young blacks and their parents. He ignited a debate even more passionate than the one Moynihan stirred: "The Outspoken Bill Cosby," cnn.com, November 11, 2004. Michael Eric Dyson gave a blistering rebuttal to Cosby in *Is Bill Cosby Right? Or Has the Black Middle Class Lost Its Mind?* (New York: Basic Books, 2005). On the other side, a number of black notables including Al Sharpton and Jesse Jackson saw some merit in Cosby's and by extension Moynihan's arguments about the black crisis: "Cosby Wins Praise for Remarks," Cox News Service, September 8, 2004.

In a presidential campaign speech on April 25, 1968, Nixon struck the old Booker T. Washington-black-economic-self-help theme when he promised by "opening new capital sources, we can help Negroes start new businesses in the ghetto and expand existing ones." *U.S. News & World Report*, September 30, 1968. It was an instant hit with the fast-increasing number of black businesses and professionals and proved to be a campaign bargaining chip for Nixon.

The GOP and even Democrats have made minority business expansion a cornerstone of their minority vote outreach strategy in the decades since Nixon blazed the way with black capitalism. Bush was only the latest in the long line of presidents and presidential candidates to pump minority business on the campaign trail in a speech to the Urban League convention: "Bush tries to sow doubts about Democrats in Urban League address," *Detroit News*, July 23, 2004.

Louis Harlan thoroughly explores Washington's laissez faire economic views in *Booker T. Washington: The Making of a Black Leader, 1856–1901* (New York: Oxford University Press, 1975). Tara Wall talked about the GOP's nonstop effort to enlist black evangelicals in "Republicans come up short courting black conservatives," *WP*, January 10, 2005.

Chapter 5 Notes
Courting the
Black Evangelicals

The leap of conservative black churchmen to make political endorsements and plunge headlong into the family values battles began in the 1980s. It took another leap forward in the 1990s, and the first years of the twenty-first century with the rise of black megachurches and their telegenic, politically shrewd leaders. The GOP quickly read the political tea leaves and recognized that they could be a big, booming voice for the party and its causes. The GOP struck pay dirt with some big-name black evangelicals in the 2004 presidential election. There was also another payoff for them in the immediate aftermath of the Katrina debacle: Bush went to the nation's best-known black evangelical, T. D. Jakes, to help in his image retooling as the compassionate conservative: "The Preacher," *Atlantic Monthly*, March 2006; "Bishop T. D. Jakes is 'Sick' Over Slow Response to Katrina." *Louisiana Weekly*, September 26, 2005.

For a good account of the fervent support Thomas got from many black evangelicals during his confirmation tussle and the current efforts of Lou Sheldon to collar black evangelicals into his Traditional Values Coalition, see "Hundreds Rally for Thomas at Start of Hearings," *People Magazine*, November 11, 1991; "African-American Pastors Urge Black Caucus To Support Marriage Amendment," traditionalvalues.org, May 27, 2004; Meyer and Abramson, *Selling Thomas*, 186-187; photo of black pastors for Thomas, *NYT*, September 11, 1991; "Black Churches Struggle Over Their Role in Politics," *NYT*, March 6, 2005.

Taylor Branch gives a detailed account of the war between King and the civil rights ministers and the conservative National Baptist Convention ministers at the black Baptists convention in 1961 in *Parting the Waters*, 504-507. During the 1960s, a number of black ministers and theologians were smitten by the rhetoric and trappings of the Black Power movement. James Cone in *A Black Theology of Liberation* (Garden City, N.Y.: Doubleday, 1973) and Gayraud Wilmore in *Black Religion and Black Radicalism: An Examination of the Black Experience in Religion* (Garden City, N.Y.: Doubleday, 1973) tell of the fight to make black churches more black-oriented. Given the conservatism of many black ministers, it was a fight that was short-lived and doomed to fail. Reagan sensed that the black Baptists were ready to support his reelection bid and quickly moved to formally get their support: "Campaign Notes; Ex-Head of Baptist Body Set to Endorse Reagan," *NYT*, September 2, 1984; "Telephone Call to Reverend T. J. Jemison" and "Meeting with Reverend T. J. Jemison & Leaders of NBCUSA," Reagan.utexas.edu/resources, September 6, 1984; September 10, 1984. The National Council of Churches ad appeared in the *NYT*, July 31, 1966.

The GOP platforms in 1980, 1984, and 1988 sounded the opening gun in the GOP's family values political campaign. Its resonance with black churchmen has been enduring since those years: presidency.ucsb.edu/site/doc/1980; 1984; 1988 platforms.

"GOP sees a Future in Black Churches," *LAT*, February 1, 2005. Polls showed substantial black pro-Thomas support at the time of his confirmation tussle: *USA Today*, July 29, 1991 and Foskett *Judging Thomas*, 231–232. Black evangelicals maintained their concern for social and economic issues in "GOP woos blacks, but faces struggle," *Detroit News*, March 27, 2005. Cummings's chide of Republicans is in "Clarence Thomas offers a glimpse of his thought," *Philadelphia Inquirer*, May 12, 2003.

The varying views of the efficacy of Bush's faith-based initiative by Robertson, Watts, and the black ministers is in "Bush, Blacks and the Faith-based Initiative," Workingforchange.com, February 23, 2005; "GOP Using Faith Initiative to Woo Voters," *WP*, September 15, 2002; "Bad Faith: Dilulio's departure highlights Bush's neglect of black churches," *American Prospect*, August 8, 2001; "Courting Black Concerns," Canadian Broadcast Corporation, CBC News Online, October 22, 2004; "A Widening Clerical and Cultural Divide over Faith-Based Funding — Blacks Find Religion in the GOP," *Fortune*, July 9, 2001; "President Highlights Faith based results at National Conference in Washington, D.C.," whitehouse.gov/news/releases, March 9, 2006. The details of and the dollar amounts shelled out for faith-based programs can be found at whitehouse,gov/government/fbci. The anti-Bush policy statements from the Congress of Black Churches cited in "Bad Faith."

Chapter 6 Notes
The Black Morals Wars

The momentous battles over the morals wars in the 1990s tipped the scales for the GOP in their weighty effort to court black evangelicals. It was really no surprise then that thousands

would turn out for Bishop Eddie Long's march to King's gravesite in Atlanta in December 2004 and that King's daughter, Bernice, would be at the forefront in the march. She was an
outspoken critic of gay marriage before and after the march:
"Interview with Bernice King," *Baptist Press News*, December 17,
2004; and allianceformarriage.org; "Gay-marriage advocates
protest King march," AP, December 11, 2004.

Long forthrightly lays out his positions on a range of issues
on his website, newbirth.org. Coretta's stinging rebuke of the
black ministers in Miami who used King's name to oppose gay
rights initiative are detailed in "Coretta Scott King Was a Vocal
Supporter of LGBT Rights," gaypeopleschronicle.com, February 3,
2006.

Black AME ministers didn't shy away from the gay marriage
issue and told why in "NAACP won't weigh gay marriage,"
Philadelphia Inquirer, July 11, 2004; "Black Support for Bush
Up According to the New Joint Center Poll," jointcenter.org/press
release/pressroom.

Black passions against gay marriage quickly translated into
voter support for anti-same sex marriage amendments, see
straightgate.net/marriagestatement10-2003, and "Bush Rewarded by Black Pastor's Faith," *LAT*, January 18, 2005. The anti-gay
comments and crusade of rapper 50 Cent, NBA star Allen
Iverson, and Reggie White are detailed in "Rapper Slurs OK,"
CNSNews.com March 17, 2004; "NBA fines player over anti-gay
slur," People for the American Way, pfaw.org 2001; "The Death
of Reggie White: An Off the Field Obituary," *Public Affairs
Magazine*, politicalaffairs.net, December 27–January, 2004. The
Pew Research Center poll surveyed American attitudes toward
homosexuality in 2005. It gave a summary of those attitudes in

the mid-1990s: "Politics and Values in a 51%–48% Nation," people-press.org, January 24, 2005.

There is an ever-expanding number of books and articles on black masculinity and black male attitudes toward gays. Two especially good works are Keith Boykins' *One More River to Cross: Black & Gay in America* (New York: Anchor Books, 1996) and Devon Carbado (ed.), *Black Men on Race, Gender, and Sexuality* (New York: New York University Press, 1999).

Sharpton and other liberal black ministers repeatedly expressed the view that gay marriage was a GOP wedge issue to get black votes. He and the ministers spoke at a black church summit on gay rights in Atlanta in February 2006. The confab was called by the black gay group, the National Black Justice Coalition: "What's Race Got to Do With It?", *The Nation*, February 13, 2006; "Meeting of minds in Atlanta — Gay, Lesbian leaders say it's past time for black religious churches to accept homosexuals into religious community," *San Francisco Chronicle*, January 19, 2006.

Fauntroy tells why he lent his name to the fight for the federal anti-gay marriage amendment in "Rare Coalition Aligns Against Gay Marriage," newhousenews.com, October 7, 2003. NAACP officials explained why they shied away from the gay marriage controversy at their convention in "NAACP won't weigh gay marriage," *Philadelphia Inquirer*, July 11, 2004. The GOP's adroit use of gay marriage as a campaign wedge issue and the crucial role it played in tilting black support to Bush in Ohio in the 2004 campaign, and the terror felt by the Democrats (such as Owens) of the GOP effort is meticulously laid out in "Bush Rewarded by Black Pastor's Faith," *LAT*, January 18, 2005; and "GOP Sees a future in Black Churches," *LAT*, February 1, 2005.

The White House meetings with Jakes; and black ministers and Rice and Bush administration officials on African development and AIDS; and GOP officials and politicians troop to Jakes's church are detailed in "Party of Lincoln wants blacks back," *USA Today*, May 12, 2005; "A U.S. Faith Initiative for Africa," *LAT*, May 29, 2005, "Black Pastors Criticize Bush on Aid to Africa," *LAT*, June 15, 2005; and "Jakes 'Sick' Over Katrina," *Louisiana Weekly*, September 26, 2005.

Chapter 7 Notes
Bashing the Icons

The appointment of Colin Powell and Condoleezza Rice to breakthrough posts in the Bush administration made them especially inviting targets for civil rights leaders, black Democrats, and many blacks. They saw their mere presence in Bush's cabinet as being tantamount to racial treason, despite their noble accolades, credentials, and accomplishments. Belafonte set the tone for the verbal bashing in his ill-famed San Diego radio interview in October 2002: "Powell: Belafonte's remark's 'unfortunate'," cnn.com, October 9, 2002; "Belafonte won't back down from Powell slave reference," cnn.com, October 14, 2002. The comments about Belafonte's remarks among blacks quickly flew hot and heavy: "House Slaves and Sacred Cows," seeblack.com, November 16, 2002; CNN Poll, cnn.com, October 9, 2002.

Belafonte was hardly original with his "house slave" rip of Powell. Decades before, Malcolm X delighted black audiences by skewering NAACP, Urban League leaders, and King as "house slaves" — and worse.

Sports, celebrity, and civil rights movement icons Jackie Robinson, Sammy Davis Jr., and Ralph Abernathy took a harsh verbal pounding from friends, associates, and many blacks for either being a Republican or endorsing the presidential bids of Nixon and Reagan. They give their painful account of the repercussions of their acts in Arnold Rampersad's *Jackie Robinson: A Biography* (New York: Knopf, 1997); Will Haygood, *In Black and White: The Life of Sammy Davis, Jr.* (New York: Knopf, 2003); and Ralph David Abernathy, *And the Walls Came Tumbling Down* (New York: Harper & Row, 1989).

Belafonte got Africare to disinvite Rice as a dinner speaker, and Conyers agreed. But there was a mild tremor when Belafonte was scheduled to speak at the Charles Schwab financial investment conference a couple of weeks later. He was not disinvited to speak, although some participants were antsy over what he'd say. The title of an *Investment News* article told their tale of jitters: "Schwab expects Impact 2002 speaker (Belafonte) to stifle political remarks: Going bananas over Belafonte," CNSNews.com/ViewNation October 24, 2002.

Even after Project 21 members got the boot from the hotel, they continued to hammer Belafonte: "Africare Dinner Sponsors Try to Mute Belafonte Controversy," CNSNews.com, October 25, 2002; "Harry Belafonte Should Apologize to Colin Powell for Racist Insults," Project 21 Press Release, nationalcenter.org, October 10, 2002. Mel Watt's nuanced criticism of Powell was in the wider context of the Democrats' blast of Bush's domestic policies in "The Bush Report Card, Part Three: Blacks at the President's

Table," blackamericaweb.com, January 30, 2005; and Powell's mid-1990s popularity, *U.S. News* poll, September 30, 1995: "The autumn of discontent: Black frustration is not confined to the police and the legal system," *U.S. News & World Report*, October 16, 1995.

Black conservative economist Walter Williams took the occasion of the Powell–Belafonte blast to correctly remind the Powell bashers that there was not nor should there be one black mindset on race; and the always-arguable point that Republican presidents had made more significant appointments of blacks than the Democrats: "Wanting Blacks to think Alike," gmu.edu/departments/economics, October 21, 2002. Jackson took his swipe at Bond and Belafonte in "HUD's Jackson talks tough on Bush administration," *New Pittsburgh Courier*, March 9, 2006.

After his resignation in November 2004, the *Washington Post* critically examined the ups and downs of Powell's tenure with the Bush administration: "Powell Announces His Resignation," *WP*, November 16, 2004. Powell also recounted his efforts on the diplomatic front in his resignation speech, "Transcript: Powell Announces His Resignation," Ibid. The instant Powell coyly hinted that he might be interested in a presidential bid, Buchanan and the ultra-right wasted no time in declaring war against him: "Why He Got Out," *Newsweek*, November 20, 1995; "Powell Media Mania, " *Extra!*, January–February, 1996.

Other than the *New York Daily News*, the press mostly ignored the in-Rice's-face attack at the expensive New York boutique and only lightly mentioned Rice being booed at the theatre: "As South drowns, Rice soaks in N.Y.," *NYDN*, September 1, 2005.

Rice's visit to the Gulf and the black churches in "Rice Defends Bush's Katrina Response," *San Francisco Chronicle*,

September 4, 2005. The Rice baiting by the Wisconsin talk show host triggered a torrent of phone calls to his and other radio talk shows for days. Following the publication of my column, "Aunt Jemima Rice, Uncle Tom Powell," on Alternet.org, November 23, 2004, the author was invited to debate the talk show host on one radio show. I declined but was informed that the talk show host went on anyway, and the calls from blacks were largely supportive of his attack.

Belafonte got in his digs at Rice, too: *USA Today*, January 21, 2003. During her confirmation hearings as secretary of state, black Republicans fought back, Interview with Ted Hayes, January 21, 2005.

Bond and Mfume's verbal broadsides at Bush and black conservatives were delivered at the NAACP convention in 2004: "NAACP Chairman Calls for Bush's Ouster," cnn.com, July 12, 2004; "Mfume calls black conservatives puppets," *Washington Times*, July 13, 2004. Mfume gave his kind-of, sort-of rebuke to the Rice bashers in an interview with blackamericaweb.com: "NAACP: Calling Rice 'Aunt Jemima' is wrong," November 22, 2004. In contrast to his "puppets" blast at Rice and black conservatives, the press only lightly reported it.

Conservatives unleashed their own verbal assault at the black namecallers of black conservatives: "How the Left Trashes Black Conservatives," frontpagemagazine.com, July 10, 2002. Interview with Julian Bond, March 1, 2006.

Dick Morris and Eileen McGann's *Condi vs. Hillary: The Next Great Presidential Race* (New York: Regan Books, 2005) provided a sketch of Rice's tour of duty as Bush's National Security Advisor and her early days as secretary of state. Richard Clarke takes his shot at Rice and the Bush White's House's 9/11 lapse in *Against All Enemies: Inside America's War on Terrorism* (New York: Free Press, 2004).

Before and after Bush's 2006 State of the Union address, blackamericaweb.com did a multi-part series on the Bush administration and black America. In interviews for the series, HUD Secretary Alphonso Jackson saw the appointments of Rice and Powell as being profoundly significant to blacks. Black Democrats still saw them as harmful to black interests. "The Bush Report Card — Part One," January 25, 2006; "Part Three," January 30, 2006, "Part Four," January 31, 2006.

Chapter 8 Notes
Katrina Dampens Bush

The backlash to President Bush's laggard response to Katrina from blacks was titanic. It threatened to unhinge the painstaking work, time, and money the GOP spent to boost black political support. It also severely wounded his image as the compassionate conservative. Bush scrambled fast to get the ship back on course in his first major post-Katrina speech in New Orleans: "Bush: 'We will do what it takes'," cnn.com, September 15, 2005.

However, the notion that Bush fiddled while the poor in New Orleans sank was confirmed months later in a damning congressional report on the administration's response to the disaster: "Katrina Response a Failure of Leadership," cnn.com, February 16, 2006; and a video that showed Bush being apprised of the potential Katrina destruction by FEMA officials but taking no action — cnn.com, "Bush Knew of Katrina's Wrath," CBSnews.com, March 1, 2006. Project 21 gave its feeble defense of Bush in "Black Group Responds to CBC Criticism of Hurricane Katrina Relief," nationalcenter.org, September 2, 2006.

Rice, meanwhile, who took heat for her seeming initial indifference to the suffering mightily defended Bush's response, and Bush also moved quickly and met with black ministers at the White House to reassure them that all was being done to aid the Katrina victims: "Katrina Pushes Issues of Race and Poverty at Bush," *WP*, September 12, 2005; "Rice Defends Bush's Katrina Response," *San Francisco Chronicle*, September 4, 2005.

With fall 2006 elections approaching, the GOP had to do spin control to ensure favorable media exposure for Blackwell, Swann, Steele, and the bumper crop of other GOP candidates: "Republican and Black: The party offers a strong field of statewide contenders," *U.S. News & World Report*, February 27, 2006; "High Hopes for New GOP Face," *LAT*, July 17, 2005; "GOP, Democrats in Its Sights, Grooms Black Candidates," *NYT*, July 1, 2005. Santorum publicly beat the Republican bushes for his antipoverty program in "Let's Deploy the Little Platoons: A Conservative Vision of Social Justice" opinionjournal.com, September 23, 2005.

The Congressional Black Caucus's persistent efforts to put forth a big, bold anti-poverty program has languished in Congress from its inception: "Congressional Black Caucus Introduces Hurricane Katrina Relief Legislation to Help Gulf Residents," civilrights.org, November 3, 2005. The CBC's effort got virtually no media attention. The possible political fallout from Katrina is assessed in "Katrina 's Aftermath, Political Landscape May Shift on Displaced Voters," *LAT,* September 11, 2005.

There were jitters among many blacks over whether Bush and the Congressional Republicans would vote to extend the Voting Rights Act in 2007: "Debate on Voting Rights Extension Begins," msnbc.msn.com, October 18, 2005. Bush put the fear to rest at his December 2005 White House press conference. He said he'd sign the VRA extension, whitehouse.gov/news, December 19, 2005; "Dean: race played role in Katrina death toll," msnbc.com, September 8, 2005.

Chapter 9 Notes
The Twenty Percent Solution

The GOP's momentary Katrina meltdown with blacks made Bush's dream of permanently bagging double-digit black support seem more remote. Bush, however, wasn't the first to hold that if Republicans could get one out of five blacks to vote for their candidates, the GOP would be the dominant party in America for decades. Republican National Committee chair Lee Atwater publicly propounded that notion in 1989: "Party of Lincoln," *The New Republic,* March 20, 1989. There were obstacles then: "The 1992 Republican 'tent': no blacks walked in," *Political Science Quarterly,* Summer 1993; "Black Republicans and 'The Speech'," *Washington Post,* November 1992.

Those same obstacles remained formidable a decade and a half later even before Katrina struck. The biggest one was still the perceived racial hostility among far too many Republicans: "Study Ties Political Leanings to Hidden Biases," *WP*, January 30, 2006. Mehlman was hardly ready to throw in the towel after Katrina. He was still very much in the hunt for increased black support: "GOP defends outreach to black voters," AP, October 11, 2005.

The GOP leanings among a small but growing number of blacks in the 1990s are detailed in "Blacks and the Republican Party," *American Prospect*, June 2005. While black Democrats and most black voters hailed Clinton as a political hero, a more sobering analysis of his presidency found that his policies on crime, the drug laws, the death penalty, welfare, and spending were more GOP-friendly than he and his supporters admitted. This was either ignored or downplayed: "Bill Clinton Was No Champion of the Poor," dissidentvoice.org, September 29, 2005. In his autobiography, *My Life*, Clinton made it clear that his domestic polices were aimed at getting white middle-class voters back to the Democratic Party (see his account of the flap with Jesse Jackson in 1992, 411-413). Jackson made his claim that he had more access to Bush than Clinton's black cabinet appointees had to Clinton in "HUD's Jackson talks tough on Bush Administration," *New Pittsburgh Courier*, March 9, 2006.

Gore also was sharply criticized during Campaign 2000 and Kerry during Campaign 2004 for their initial refusal to put social issues on the front burner in their campaigns and pose a solid alternative to Bush's policies: "Bradley challenges Gore on racial profiling," AP, January 17, 2000; "The 2000 Campaign: Sharpton Seeks Debate on Race Issues," *NYT*, February 7, 2000; "Kerry Campaign Chided on Diversity," *Washington Times*, May 5, 2004.

Bush's White House meeting with black ministers and his assurance that GOP policies are conducive to blacks: "Bush continues outreach to blacks," *Washington Times*, February 9, 2005. Sowell and Connerly were having none of Bush's Democratic-lite racial maneuvers: "Republicans and Blacks," gopusa.com/commentary/sowell, January 30, 2006; Ward Connerly correspondence with author, March 27, 2006.

Notes
Postscript

When Bush threw down the gauntlet to the Democrats at the Urban League Convention in 2004, he was truly on a roll. His admonition to the delegates that the Democrats had taken blacks for granted resonated with them: "Bush tries to sow doubts about Democrats in Urban League address," *Detroit News*, July 26, 2004.

The Democratic National Committee voiced its concern over GOP racial thrust in "GOP drive to woo blacks via church alarms Brazile," *WP*, March 3, 2005.

Bibliography

Amaker, Norman C. *Civil Rights and the Reagan Administration* (Washington, D.C.: Urban Institute Press, 1988)

Ball, Howard. *A Defiant Life — Thurgood Marshall & The Persistence of Racism in America* (New York: Crown Books, 1998)

Barone, Michael. *The Shaping of America From Roosevelt to Reagan* (New York: Free Press, 1990)

The Black Scholar (editors). *Court of Appeal: The Black Community Speaks out on The Racial and Sexual Politics of Thomas vs. Hill* (New York: Ballantine Books, 1992)

Boykin, Keith. *One More River to Cross: Black & Gay in America* (New York: Anchor Books, 1996)

Brisbin, Richard A. *Justice Antonin Scalia and the Conservative Revival* (Baltimore: Johns Hopkins University Press, 1998)

Branch, Taylor. *Parting the Waters: America in the King Years 1954–63* (New York: Simon & Schuster, 1988)

_____. *Pillar of Fire: America in the King Years 1963–1965* (New York: Simon & Schuster, 1998)

_____. *At Canaan's Edge: America in the King Years, 1965–1968* (New York: Simon & Schuster, 2006)

Burk, Robert Frederick. *The Eisenhower Administration and Black Civil Rights* (Knoxville: University of Tennessee Press, 1984)

183

Bush, George W., and Mickey Herskowitz. *A Change to Keep: My Journey to the White House* (New York, HarperCollins, 2001)

Carbado, Devon W. (ed.). *Black Men on Race, Gender, and Sexuality* (New York: New York University Press, 1999)

Cannon, Lou. *President Reagan: The Role of a Lifetime* (New York: Simon & Schuster, 1991)

Carter, Dan T. *The Politics of Rage: George Wallace: The Origins of the New Conservatism and the Transformation of American Politics* (New York: Simon & Schuster, 1995)

Carter, Jimmy. *Keeping Faith: Memoirs of a President* (New York: Bantam Books, 1982)

Clarke, Richard A. *Against all Enemies: Inside America's War on Terrorism* (New York: Free Press, 2004)

Clinton, Bill. *My Life* (New York: Knopf, 2004)

Columbus, Salley, and Walter Fauntroy. *What Color is Your God: Black Consciousness and the Christian Faith* (Seacaucus, N.J.: Citadel, 1988)

Connerly, Ward. *Creating Equal: My Fight Against Race Preferences* (San Francisco: Encounter Books, 2002)

Conrad, Cecilia A., et al. *African-Americans in the U.S. Economy* (Lanham, Md.: Rowan & Littlefield, 2005)

Constantine-Simms, Delroy (ed.). *The Greatest Taboo: Homosexuality in Black Communities* (Los Angeles: Alyson Publications, 2000)

Curry, George (ed.). *The Affirmative Action Debate* (New York: Addison-Wesley, 1996)

Daniels, Ronald J. (ed.), et al. *On Risk and Disasters: Lessons From Hurricane Katrina* (Harrisburg, Pa.: University of Pennsylvania Press, 2006)

Dean, Howard, and Judith Warner. *You Have the Power: How to Take Back Our Country and Restore Democracy in America* (New York: Simon & Schuster, 2004)

Denton, Robert E., Jr. (ed.). *2004 Presidential Campaign: A Communication Perspective* (Lanham, Md.: Rowman & Littlefield Publishers, 2005)

_____. *2000 Presidential Campaign: A Communication Perspective* (Westport, Ct.: Praeger Publishers, 2002)

Diamond, Sara. *Roads to Dominion: Right-Wing Movements and Political Power in America* (New York: Guilford, 1995)

Dyson, Michael Eric. *Is Bill Cosby Right? Or Has the Black Middle Class Lost Its Mind?* (New York: Basic Books, 2005)

_____. *Come Hell or High Water: Hurricane Katrina and the Color of Disaster* (New York: Perseus Books, 2006)

Felix, Antonia. *Condi: The Condoleezza Rice Story* (New York: New Market, 2005)

Foskett, Ken. *Judging Thomas* (New York: Harper-Collins Publishers, 2004)

Franklin, Robert M. *Another Day's Journey: Black Churches Confronting the American Crisis* (Minneapolis: Augsburg Fortress Publishers, 1991)

Frazier, E. Franklin. *Black Bourgeoisie* (Glencoe, Ill.: Free Press, 1957)

_____. *The Negro Family in the United States* (Chicago: University of Chicago Press, 1966)

_____. *The Negro Church in America* (New York: Schocken Books, 1966)

Glasgow, Douglas G. *The Black Underclass: Poverty, Unemployment and Entrapment of Ghetto Youth* (New York: Vintage Books, 1980)

Hacker, Andrew. *Two Nations: Black and White, Separate, Hostile, Unequal* (New York: Macmillan Books, 1992)

Hardisty, Jean. *Mobilizing Resentment: Conservative Resurgence from the John Birch Society to the Promise Keepers* (Boston: Beacon Press, 1999)

Harlan, Louis. *Booker T. Washington: The Making of a Black Leader, 1856–1901* (New York: Oxford University Press, 1975)

Harper, Phillip Brian. *Are We Not Men? Masculine Anxiety and the Problem of African-American Identity* (New York: Oxford University Press, 1996)

Higginbotham, A. Leon. *Shades of Freedom: Racial Politics and the Presumption of the American Legal Process* (New York: Oxford University Press, 1996)

Johnson, John H., and Lerone Bennett, Jr. *Succeeding Against the Odds* (Boston: Warner Books, 1989)

Olasky, Marvin. *Compassionate Conservatism: What It is, What It Does, and How It Can Transform America* (New York: Free Press, 2000)

O'Reilly, Kenneth. *Nixon's Piano: Presidents and Racial Politics From Washington to Clinton* (New York: Free Press, 1995)

Phillips, Kevin. *The Politics of Rich and Poor: Wealth and the American Electorate in the Reagan Aftermath* (New York: Random House, 1990)

Pincus, Fred L. (ed.). *Race and Ethnic Conflict* (Boulder, Co.: Westview Press, 1994)

Powell, Colin. *My American Journey* (New York: Ballantine Books, 1996)

Raskin, Jamin R. *Overruling Democracy: The Supreme Court versus the American People* (New York: Routledge, 2003)

Reagan, Ronald. *An American Life* (New York: Simon & Schuster, 1990)

Reese, Renford. *American Paradox: Young Black Men* (Durham, N.C.: Carolina Academic Press, 2004)

Robertson, Pat. *The New World Order* (Dallas: World Publishing Group, 1991)

Sammon, Bill. *Strategery: How George W. Bush Is Defeating Terrorist,. Outwitting Democrats, and Confounding the Mainstream Media* (New York: Regnery, 2006)

Schuyler, George. *Black and Conservative* (New Rochelle, N.Y.: Arlington House, 1966)

Skinner, Kiron D. *Reagan in His Own Hand: The Writings of Ronald Reagan that Reveal His Revolutionary Vision for America* (New York: Free Press, 2001)

Simon, Roger. *Divided We Stand: How Al Gore beat George Bush and Lost the Presidency* (New York: Crown, 2001)

Sowell, Thomas. *Civil Rights: Rhetoric or Reality?* (New York: William Morrow, 1984)

_____. *Black Rednecks and White Liberals* (New York: Encounter Books, 2005)

_____. *The Fairmont Papers* — Black Alternatives Conference (San Francisco: Institute for Contemporary Studies, 1981)

Steele, Shelby. *The Content of Our Character: A New Vision of Race in America* (New York: St. Martins Press, 1990)

Stefanci, Jean, and Robert Delgado. *No Mercy: How Conservative Think Tanks and Foundations Changed America's Social Agenda* (Philadelphia: Temple University Press, 1998)

Washington, James M. A. *Testament of Hope: The Essential Writings and Speeches of Martin Luther King, Jr.* (New York: HarperCollins, 1986

Watts, J. C. *What Color Is a Conservative: My Life and My Politics* (New York: Perennial Press, 2003)

Weyrich, Paul. *Future 21: Directions for America in the 21st Century* (Greenwich, Ct.: Devin-Adair Publishing, 1984)

White, Reggie. *Broken Promises, Blended Dreams, Taking Charge of Your Destiny* (Shippensburg, Pa.; Destiny Image Publishers, 2003)

Williams, Armstrong. *How We Can Succeed by Breaking the Dependency Barrier* (New York: Free Press, 1995)

Wilmore, Gayraud. *Black Religion and Black Radicalism: An Examination of the Black Experience in Religion* (Garden City, N.Y.: Doubleday, 1973)

Woodward, Bob. *Plan of Attack* (New York: Simon & Schuster, 2004)

Index